OTHER SEXES

*Rewriting Difference from
Woolf to Winterson*

Andrea L. Harris

STATE UNIVERSITY
OF NEW YORK PRESS

Published by
State University of New York Press, Albany

Printed in the United States of America

For information, address the State University of New York Press,
State University Plaza, Albany, NY 12246

Marketing by Patrick Durocher • Production by Bernadine Dawes

Library of Congress Cataloging-in-Publication Data

Harris, Andrea L., 1962–
    Other sexes: rewriting difference from Woolf to Winterson /
Andrea L. Harris.
       p.   cm. — (SUNY series in feminist criticism and theory)
    Includes bibliographical references (p.) and index.
    ISBN 0-7914-4455-4 (hc : alk. paper). — ISBN 0-7914-4456-2 (pb :
alk. paper)
    1. English fiction—Women authors—History and criticism.
2. Feminism and literature—Great Britain—History—20th century.
3. Feminism and literature—United States—History—20th century.
4. Winterson, Jeanette, 1959– —Criticism and interpretation.
6. American fiction—Women authors—History and criticism.
7. Hauser, Marianne—Criticism and interpretation. 9. Difference (Psychology) in
literature. 10. Gender identity in literature. 11. Sex role in
literature. I. Title. II. Series.
PR 888.F45H37 2000
823′.91099287—dc21   99-23584
                                                        CIP

1   2   3   4   5   6   7   8   9   10

For Felice and Sofia

CONTENTS

ACKNOWLEDGMENTS

My work on this book was funded in part by a grant from the State System of Higher Education of Pennsylvania, for which I am grateful. The people who have helped in various ways with this project make up a small but important group. For their help at an earlier stage in this project, I am indebted to Stacy Hubbard, Susan Eilenberg, and Henry Sussman. For insightful comments on the complete manuscript, I am grateful to Laura Doan. Linda Dunleavy, Lycette Nelson, and John Ulrich gave excellent advice on drafts of various chapters, for which I thank them. For always supporting me and for much else, I owe a great deal to my family, especially my mother, Friede Harris, and my sister, Christina Harris Thurston. For generous support and friendship, I want to thank Linda Dunleavy, Lycette Nelson, Nina Panzer, and Louise Sullivan-Blum. For always seeing me through and for making me laugh, I give many thanks to Felice Reitknecht. Finally, for being her amazing, sweet self, I thank my daughter, Sofia.

Portions of this book first appeared in the following publications: "'Bare Things': Returning to the Senses in Virginia Woolf's *The Waves.*" *LIT: Literature, Interpretation, Theory* 7.4 (1997); "This difference . . . this identity . . . was overcome': Merging Masculine and Feminine in Virginia Woolf's *The Waves.*" *Virginia Woolf and the Arts: Selected Papers from the Sixth Annual Conference on Virginia Woolf.* Ed. Diane F. Gillespie and Leslie K. Hankins. New York: Pace University Press, 1997; "'The Third Sex': Figures of Inversion in Djuna Barnes's *Nightwood.*" *GENDERS 20: Eroticism and Containment: Notes from the Flood Plain.* Ed. Carol Siegel and Ann Kibbey. New York: New York University Press, 1994. I am grateful to the publishers for permission to reprint.

PREFACE

> It would be a thousand pities if women wrote like men, or lived like men, or looked like men, for if two sexes are quite inadequate, considering the vastness and variety of the world, how should we manage with one only? Ought not education to bring out and fortify the differences rather than the similarities? For we have too much likeness as it is, and if an explorer should come back and bring word of other sexes looking through the branches of other trees at other skies, nothing would be of greater service to humanity . . .
>
> —Virginia Woolf, *A Room of One's Own*

> If sexual difference is to be overcome is it not imperative first of all to find a sexual ethics? If one day we are to be one must we not now be *two*? Otherwise we fall back into some formal and empty *(male) one*, back into the hierarchies we are familiar with . . .
>
> —Luce Irigaray, *Sexes and Genealogies*

Nearly sixty years of writing and theorizing on the subject of women divide Virginia Woolf and Luce Irigaray, and yet their ideas about sexual difference in these passages have much in common. Both thinkers insist that we need more difference in order to reach a point beyond difference. Or, as Woolf states, we need to "fortify the differences" since "we have too much likeness as it is." My aim here is also to "fortify the differences" by analyzing texts by a particular group of twentieth-century women novelists that question the way in which the sex/gender binary works to conceal rather than reveal difference. Woolf's notion of "other sexes" is simply remarkable: in Western culture, our very notions of love, reproduction, and even humanness are firmly grounded in the "fact" that there are two sexes, the male and the female. To casually suggest, as Woolf does, that there may be "other sexes" out there strikes me as a subversive and irresistible challenge. I borrow Woolf's phrase "other sexes" in order to point to the ways in which certain texts by women pose a distinct threat to the prevailing concept of sexual difference. For the notions of both sex and gender are binary: to speak of a "third sex," as Barnes does, or of "other sexes," as Woolf does, is already to begin the work of dismantling the system in which both sex (conceived as anatomical or biological) and gender (conceived as social or cultural) are made to fit into two discrete and narrow categories.[1] My project here is to explore the various ways in which women writers—both theorists and novelists—explore the border between masculine and feminine, in other words, the place where these terms overlap and intersect, forming other sexes that cannot be described with the language at our disposal. This exploration involves crossing the boundary between masculine and feminine in order to discover genuine sexual difference.

My choice of texts also involves a crossing of conventional boundaries. I bring together here the canonical modernist author Virginia Woolf and with her contemporary Djuna Barnes, who does not figure in the standard American modernist canon. Woolf's *The Waves*, the subject of my second chapter, is one of her most neglected novels, probably because it is widely perceived as difficult, and occasionally perceived as a failure. Barnes's *Nightwood*, the subject of chapter 3, is also a "difficult" text: critically neglected for years, it has been celebrated lately in the Barnes revival of the 1980s and 1990s, but it is still not a fixture in the classroom or in academic journals. I then move from modernism to postmodernism, with Marianne Hauser's 1976 American novel *The Talking Room* as the focus of chapter 4. Hauser's remarkable novel has yet to receive wide readership and critical attention, although it is richly deserving of both.[2] In my final chapter, I return to the British novel—Jeanette Winterson's *Written on the Body*. Winterson, unlike Hauser, is widely known and quite popular, but there is not as yet a large body of criticism on her work. Since Winterson infamously claims to be a latter-day Woolf, my study comes full circle. To a certain extent my choice of these novels arose by chance. When I first read *Nightwood*, I was astonished by Barnes's radical questioning of sex and gender through her figures of the invert, and I began to see the same sort of gender disruption in other novels by women. Reading *The Talking Room* soon after *Nightwood*, the original idea for this book began to take shape, since I saw Hauser's novel as describing a similar but more radical upheaval of the gender binary. My work on these American texts began to influence my reading of *The Waves*, and I turned my focus to gender in that text. The nongendered narrator of *Written on the Body* made this novel an obvious choice for my study. The germ of my critical framework has evolved from my readings of the novels in many ways. Judith Butler's model of performative gender and Luce Irigaray's concept of the sensible transcendental break down binary gender in such a way as to make "other sexes" possible. This title, "other sexes," strikes me a perfect phrase to describe the variously sexed / gendered subjects that people the novels of Woolf, Barnes, Hauser, and Winterson. Following an introductory chapter on feminist theory and gender studies, I have arranged the chapters on the novels chronologically, an ordering that also makes theoretical sense. From Woolf onward, the questioning of sex/gender takes on a greater force. While Woolf and Barnes tend to question and destabilize gender through strategies of displacement and inversion, Hauser thoroughly disrupts and undermines gender through performance and Winterson gestures toward a state beyond gender. From Woolf to Winterson, gender is redefined as a series of shifting, fluid identifications, rather than a narrowly conceived static opposition. At the same time and through the same textual moves, language is restored to its original grounding in the body—thus, its original configuration as feminine.

The original title of this book was *The Third Sex*, referring to a term coined in the nineteenth century to designate the concept of the homosexual as a man trapped in a woman's body.[3] The term was appropriated by Barnes in *Nightwood*, in which "the third sex" is rewritten to refer to a creature of ambiguous, shifting, and heightened gender.[4] I initially found "the third sex" a perfect term to refer to the ways in which women writers attempt to revise the prevailing system of binary gender. In order to question this hierarchy, it is necessary to posit a third term as a way to move beyond opposition. But a third term or a "third sex" implies a stopping place, while "other sexes" implies the beginning of a series. "Other sexes" alludes to all that is excluded and repressed by the limited either/or opposition of masculine/feminine in a way that "the third sex" cannot.

What is the common territory of the novels that I study here? Beginning with almost superficial resemblances, the narrative of each text centers around or issues from a woman or a figure of woman. These women are also linked with "feminine" qualities: silence, beauty, and the body. At the same time, they are linked with masculine qualities: the production of meaning, storytelling, and active sexuality. These women lack a clear-cut identity and are known paradoxically by their very lack of identity. In privileging and voiding this feminine space that is central to the narrative, the texts mime the position of woman in masculinist discourse as the empty object of representation. Yet the repetition, the mime, does not mean pure duplication but repetition with a difference: anonymity is not mere lack of identity but multiplicity of identity, and the notion of identity itself is questioned and emptied out. The various novels "use" the privileged feminine to different ends.[5] This might involve uncovering or recovering a buried feminine that does not resemble the feminine of phallogocentric discourse or using the feminine in order to subvert binary gender and to question the stability of the terms masculine and feminine. Despite these differences, the goals and the outcomes of these various feminist textual projects greatly resemble each other. The common goal is to move beyond the narrow constraints of one gender or the fiction of two genders, since the same/other structure of a binary opposition means that essentially there is only one. This movement beyond into the true realm of otherness (not the other as flip side of the same, but the other as truly and radically other) involves, in each of these texts, a movement across borders and boundaries of all kinds. In many instances, the oppositions between concepts are crossed, if not crisscrossed. The line that demarcates terms is naturalized as representing an inherent or essential difference, but the process of violating this line reveals that it in fact constructs difference. These texts thus enact the undoing of opposition by exploring the other, the third, the intermediary, the boundary, the border, and the fluid. In one way or another, all the texts rewrite difference by inhabiting the space of the between where seeming opposites come together. The forms of these boundary crossings are various: dissonance between sex, gender identity, and sexual practice; the meeting and inversion of genders in the subject; and butch-femme lesbian styles. While gender is represented in fiction in the form of characters in the most obvious sense, it is also deeply embedded in the text's style. I argue that gender and style form the central connection between feminism and modernity: what is most experimental about these novels is the central placing of gender and the way in which gender questioning is at the heart of the style. Feminist theorists such as Irigaray and Butler and feminist novelists such as Woolf, Barnes, Hauser, and Winterson make us see that the complexity of gender is not adequately conveyed by masculine and feminine, for these terms do not begin to suggest the intricate interplay between the genders, both within the subject and within language. Woolf's suggestive phrase, "other sexes," has the advantage of implying just this, that sex/gender consists of an open-ended series of possibilities.

ONE

(RE)PLACING THE FEMININE
IN FEMINIST THEORY

One of the key theoretical debates of the 1990s in literary studies is the question of the relationship between the relatively new field of gay and lesbian studies, most specifically queer theory, and feminist theory. The fast-growing discipline of gay and lesbian studies seeks to distinguish itself by claiming its difference from feminism, especially the difference of the object of study.[1] While gender is the domain of feminism, say many gay and lesbian studies scholars, sexuality is the domain of gay and lesbian studies. This critical move has itself received critical attention in articles by Judith Butler and Biddy Martin.[2] These critics argue that the debt of gay and lesbian studies to feminism is a large one, but more importantly, that there is a distinct danger in severing the relation between sexuality and gender in our critical endeavors.[3] How has this divide between feminism and lesbian and gay studies come about in literary theory in the past twenty years? What are the connections between these fields of study? How might we get beyond seeing these fields as divided by reading literary texts by women that engage similar issues? The first chapter of this book attempts to engage in this debate by returning to the work of some of the key figures in these fields, and subsequent chapters do so by turning to literary texts by women in order to see the ways in which gender and sexuality, and what I would argue is their inevitable connection, are similarly explored in literature.

In order to argue for this inevitable connection between gender and sexuality, I will turn first to a selection of texts from the 1970s and 1980s that may be loosely grouped under the heading "deconstructive feminism." I want to compare different placings of the feminine in theoretical discourse in order to show that even when the feminine seems to be the privileged term of a text, it may be a displacement of the feminine that is operating there. The displacement of the feminine comes about through a failure to acknowledge its specificity, or, to use an Irigarayan metaphor, the failure to unearth the buried feminine upon which masculine discourse is founded. Another aspect of displacement is the male philosopher/theorist's appropriation of the feminine for his own ends, as analyzed by Gayatri Chakravorty Spivak. I will begin with Alice Jardine's model of "gynesis," which attempts to account for the privileging of woman in modernity, but involves a displacement of woman. I will then turn to Jacques Derrida's remarks in interviews on the place of woman in deconstruction and as well as Spivak's reading of Derrida. We need to look first at displacement because it is the impetus for feminism: displacement is the appropriation of woman for masculinist ends. For a model to counter displacement, I will also look briefly at the history of the term "mimesis," which we might call the employment of the feminine for feminist ends. Irigaray's concept of mimesis, a term with a complex and long history within feminism, refocuses attention on the feminine and its potential for subversion.[4] In Irigaray's writings, the feminine itself possesses textual power; the feminine is not merely "privileged" by the male subject, as in gynesis. Irigaray's feminine stands for the point of impossibility of masculine discourse and the negative image of the male subject, and she draws attention to the spots where masculine discourse must work hard to keep the feminine at bay, due to its disruptive, dismantling power.

The emphasis on play and masquerade in mimesis will serve as a bridge to Judith Butler's theory of performative gender, which shifts the focus from the feminine exclusively to gender more broadly. Performativity and mimesis share much territory, but performativity is not exclusively the property of the feminine as mimesis is, since Butler conceives of masculinity as performative as well. After considering the social constructivist strand in feminist theory represented by Butler's work, I will turn again to Irigaray, in this case her later work (published in France in the mid-1980s but appearing in English translation in the early 1990s). Texts such as *Sexes and Genealogies* and *An Ethics of Sexual Difference* offer ways around the seeming impasse in the debate over the role of feminist theory in newer discourses of sexuality and gender. In this more recent work, Irigaray develops the concept of the "sensible transcendental." As the name implies, this concept involves a meeting of oppositionally defined terms. The coming together of sensible and transcendental works to heal the split between feminine and masculine, which, for Irigaray, is a restoration of an originary connection. While Irigaray posits this as the path to a true recognition of sexual difference, I would argue that we end up not with true femininity and true masculinity but with a meeting of the genders within each sex. Butler's model of gender performance captures this destabilizing of the masculine/feminine hierarchy. This meeting of the genders within each sex would be the "other sexes" of my title, in which male and female, masculinity and femininity, are both present, and, as a result, genuine sexual difference is fully realized.

Gynesis and Displacement: Configurations of the Feminine

In her 1985 book *Gynesis: Configurations of Woman and Modernity*, Alice Jardine focuses on representations of the feminine in male-authored poststructuralist, postmodernist writing (which Jardine terms the writing of "modernity"). Jardine's aim is to unearth the importance of the feminine in modernity and to show how the feminine may be the crucial term on which modernity itself depends. Jardine defines "gynesis" as "the putting into discourse of 'woman' as that *process* diagnosed in France as intrinsic to the condition of modernity; indeed, the valorization of the feminine, woman, and her obligatory, that is, historical[,] connotations, as somehow intrinsic to new and necessary modes of thinking, writing, speaking" (25; emphasis in original). Gynesis seems closely related to mimesis, for it involves privileging the feminine's "historical connotations," such as body, nature, passivity, matter, other, etc.[5] It is precisely these obligatory connotations of the feminine that make the model of gynesis problematic. Other "obligatory . . . historical" connotations of the feminine, such as difference, multiplicity, and excess, are more potentially disruptive and subversive. For this reason, these qualities are suppressed in phallogocentric discourse and they also seem to be suppressed in the texts of modernity examined by Jardine. Privileging multiplicity, for example, is more potentially disruptive than privileging passivity. Furthermore, to keep insisting on certain defining characteristics of the feminine and the masculine drives home the structure of binary gender rather than challenging it. Only when the end result of privileging the feminine is the questioning of gender norms can such a strategy be considered a feminist one.

Where mimesis and gynesis differ primarily is in application. Jardine studies male-authored texts exclusively, and these texts often involve the male subject usurping the place of woman for his own.[6] Woman in a sense has no "place" in gynesis. In mimesis, by contrast, the feminine is privileged by and for the feminine. In fact, Jardine writes that she is "more concerned about the *process* of (reading and writing) woman than about examining the representation of women in literature" (19; emphasis in original). This concern may lead her to avoid women in other respects, for example, the work of other women theorists. Anticipating the feminist response to this (why read Derrida and Lacan rather than Irigaray and Cixous?), Jardine explains that the female theorists are "direct disciples of those men" (21). The implication is that she must go to the primary source and thus align herself as a direct disciple of the male theorists, rather than align herself as a disciple of a disciple. So, Irigaray, Cixous, and Julia Kristeva are set up as secondary to the men, as disciples.[7] A related problem is that the connection between "woman" and women is often severed completely in gynetic texts. Although Jardine expresses concern for maintaining this connection, it is difficult to see this concern played out, given her ambivalent relation to women as theorists and subjects.[8] Acknowledging this very lack of connection between woman and women, Jardine writes that in gynetic texts, "woman may become intrinsic to entire conceptual systems, without [these systems] being 'about' women—much less 'about' feminism" (61). Certainly, the fact that these conceptual systems are not "about" women, does not pose a problem when taken at face value. However, these systems use the concept of the feminine or attributes of the feminine in certain strategic ways, for certain nonfeminist aims.[9] For a feminist, the connection between woman and women, however distant or problematic it is, must be reinstated.

To "privilege woman," the basis of Jardine's concept of gynesis, does not necessarily represent a feminist move, particularly if the concept of woman is disconnected from women in the world. In order to demonstrate this, I will compare the privileging of woman in a text by Derrida with the privileging of woman in the concept of "mimesis" in Irigaray's texts. In the former, the woman is "desexualized," according to Derrida: the hymen of "The Double Session" is a metaphor; the "invagination" of "Living On/Border-lines" is also a metaphor. Desexualized, these terms no longer refer to the system of heterosexual exchange by which women are traded (what Irigaray calls "hom(m)o-sexuality" [*This Sex* 171]), nor do they even refer to female anatomy. In Irigaray's texts, by contrast, a term such as "the lips" is anything but desexualized; we might even say it is hypersexualized. Irigaray takes the fact that the two sets of lips of the female body are unique to it and exploits them for their subversive potential. Derrida, by contrast, appropriates such terms in the sense that he cuts off their connection to femininity (or, at least, he attempts to do so).

Derrida's use of the term "hymen" raises the issue of woman being "intrinsic to entire conceptual systems without [these systems] being 'about' women—much less 'about' feminism" (*Gynesis* 61). It also brings up the woman/women division, which for feminism must be seen instead as a connection. Derrida's remarks on the hymen in "Choreographies," an interview, bear directly on this problem. Christie McDonald, the interviewer, notes that both "hymen" and "invagination" "pertain in their most widely recognized sense to the woman's body" ("Choreographies" 74). Marking her "careful formulation," appropriate because of the rarity of sexualized terms in philosophical discourse, Derrida claims that with these terms, he has deliberately "resexualized" a discourse that has always "neutralized" itself in respect to sexual difference. However, even as Derrida grants that these terms are sexualized, he insists that they cannot be simply attributed to the female body. In this way, he both resexualizes and desexualizes discourse at the same time. Derrida remarks:

> "[H]ymen" and "invagination," at least in the context into which those words have been swept, no longer simply designate figures for the feminine body . . . One could say quite accurately that the hymen *does not exist*. Anything constituting the value of existence

is foreign to the "hymen" . . . How can one then attribute the
existence of the hymen *properly* to woman? Not that it is any more
the distinguishing feature of man, or for that matter, of the human creature. (75; emphasis in original)

Just as he does with the trace (*Of Grammatology* 65) and *différance*
(*Margins* 6, 14–15), Derrida makes it impossible to attribute femininity to the hymen by stating that the hymen does not exist.
According to this logic, woman—or, rather, parts of her dismem-
bered body—is intrinsic to "The Double Session" and to "Living
On/Border Lines," yet these texts are not about woman, women,
or feminism in any way. Not only are these texts not about women,
but the very terms "hymen" and "invagination" cannot be called
feminine metaphors according to Derrida's qualifications.

To claim that the hymen "does not exist," in the sense that it
does not refer to the body because its referential status is suspended, is a standard Derridean maneuver. In other words, Derrida
attempts to recontextualize it so that it refers to a material configuration rather than to a sexed body in the world.[10] If nothing
else, necessity dictates this, for the term, like the trace, must be
thought outside of metaphysical conceptuality. Nevertheless,
"hymen" and "invagination" are not neutral, desexualized terms:
they do refer, if only in "their most widely recognized sense," to
the female body. Yet if Derrida were to speak of the hymen as per-
taining to women, would these texts be equally problematic for
feminism? The answer is yes. The hymen links woman to marriage as a system of exchange and to heterosexuality exclusively.
Thus, metaphor or not, the hymen is not a likely place from which
to launch a feminist discourse. By stating that the hymen does not
refer to the female body, Derrida effaces and subsequently appropriates the figure of woman, a move analyzed by Spivak. As in
Jardine's study, Spivak's subject in her essay "Displacement and
the Discourse of Woman" is the way in which the figure of woman
is privileged in Derrida's texts. But Spivak pushes the analysis
further, questioning why much of Derrida's work seems to hinge
on woman, and how the figure of woman is privileged. Spivak
begins with a juxtaposition of Western discourse as a centrism
(logo-, phallo-, etc.) and of deconstructive discourse as a displacement, or decentering of this centrism.[11] According to Spivak,

Derrida stresses the fact that the subject is "irreducibly displaced"; however, "in a discourse that privileges the center, women alone have been diagnosed as such; correspondingly, he attempts to displace all centrisms, binary oppositions, or centers" (170). Derrida, then, privileges woman because she is displaced from the start: woman has traditionally stood in for the displacement of all subjects. This is another way of saying that woman is other to man's same, or that woman constitutes sexual difference as such. While the system of deconstruction depends on the figure of woman, woman is also that which the system cannot pin down.

Given that woman is constituted as an originary displacement in phallocentric discourse, what happens to this figure in deconstructive discourse, which attempts to decenter the former? Spivak argues that Derrida's textual operation displaces the woman yet again, thus reenacting the primary displacement. The opening of *Spurs* provides the model for this double displacement ("Displacement" 171). There Derrida writes, "Woman will be my subject"— "subject here meaning both the topic of discourse and the philosophical "I." That is, Derrida will both speak of woman and speak from the place (the dis-placed place) of the woman. In Spivak's words,

> [T]he author . . . having stepped into the place of displacement, has displaced the woman-model doubly as shuttling between the author's subject and object . . . we are already in the circuit of what I call double displacement: in order to secure the gesture of taking the woman as model, the figure of woman must be doubly displaced. (171)

Derrida's "use" of the hymen operates similarly. He privileges it because two of its attributes—materiality and undecidability— make it a natural choice as a metaphor for Derridean writing. But, at the same time, he severs the connection between hymen and women, that is, the "origin" of the hymen in the female body. Analyzing Derrida's use of the hymen as metaphor, Spivak first describes the hymen's figurative and literal status: "'metaphorically' it is the ritual celebration of the breaking of the vaginal membrane, and 'literally' that membrane remains intact even as it opens up into two lips; second, the walls of the passage that houses the

hymen are both inside and outside the body" (74). The duplicity
and undecidability of the hymen make it ripe for Derrida's pick-
ing: the hymen is broken, yet intact; one membrane, yet two lips;
inside the body, yet outside it as well. In reading the hymen further, Spivak uncovers the implications behind Derrida's choice of
female body part. She writes:

> Is there not an agenda unwittingly concealed in formulating *vir-
> ginity* as the property of the sexually undisclosed challenger of
> the phallus as master of the dialectics of desire? The hymen is of
> course at once both itself and not-itself, always operated by a
> calculated dissymmetry rather than a mere contradiction or rec-
> onciliation. Yet if the one term of the dissymmetry is virginity,
> the other term is marriage, legal certification for appropriation
> in the interest of the passage of property. (74; emphasis in original)

This passage makes it clear that the hymen is anything but an innocent, neutral term signifying "only" a certain material configuration, as Derrida would have us think.[12] If anyone should insist
on the multiple meanings that one word may put into play, it
should be Derrida, but with the hymen he uncharacteristically limits its signifying capabilities. The hymen is then privileged as a
key term in his discourse with the provision that it no longer
refers to sexuality or to the female body. That is, the woman is
expunged from the scene of writing and only one of her body parts,
which is no longer properly hers, remains behind. By eliminating
woman through the appropriation of the hymen, Derrida's text
remains firmly situated within a phallogocentric economy, since
the hymen is the mark of woman as man's property. Once the
hymen is broken, a woman's value as property, as goods, diminishes. Moreover, the hymen in Derrida's text is the mark of the
feminization of the text, and, thus, of the feminization of the male
subject, which is based on the elimination of the woman.

Because this secondary displacement of woman in deconstructive discourse is a reenactment of the primary displacement of
woman in phallogocentric discourse, the privileging of woman
that goes along with the double displacement must be read especially critically, as Spivak does. She juxtaposes the two displace-
ments in this way:

[T]he deconstructive discourse of man (like the phallogocentric one) can declare its own displacement (as the phallogocentric its placing) by taking the woman as object or figure. When Derrida suggests that Western discourse is caught within the metaphysical or phallogocentric limit, his point is precisely that man can problematize but not fully disown his status as subject. (173)

This passage seems to imply that woman, in comparison to man, is already barred from subjecthood from the start. In Western discourse, according to Spivak and Irigaray, this is the case, since all theories of "the subject" are constructed in reference to the male subject. What is important in Spivak's analysis of Derrida is that she uncovers the connection between the apparent "privileging" of woman in deconstructive discourse and the blatant subordination of woman in phallogocentric discourse. The connection is this: the deconstructive philosopher wants to question or problematize his status as subject, so he must take woman's lack of subjectivity in phallogocentric discourse, claim it as his own, and privilege it. The specific nature of this privileging of the feminine is also examined: not only are certain attributes associated with the feminine now privileged (undecidability, materiality, etc.) but the very place of the woman in conceptual systems is privileged as well. Moreover, this is the nonplace on which the system is built and from which the male philosopher now speaks. Just as woman is the matter upon which Western philosophy is founded (as analyzed in Irigaray's *Speculum*) and the blind spot at which psychoanalysis cannot stop looking in vain (also in *Speculum*), so certain texts in Derrida's corpus (and other modern "gynetic" texts) are erected on the spot where the doubly displaced woman once stood. Following Spivak's line of argument, Derrida's remarks that the hymen must be thought outside of metaphysical conceptuality may be read as an attempt to conceal the double displacement operating here, a fact that is crucial for feminists to understand.

In "Women in the Beehive," a dialogue with students included in *Men in Feminism*, Derrida is asked about the place of woman in his work and seems to give some direct answers to the question. Woman is one of the terms for "originary undecidability" (a term the questioner borrowed from Spivak), because, Derrida says, "the side of the woman is the side from which you start to dismantle the structure" in the context of European phallogocentrism (194). But using woman in this process of dismantling is only appropriate through the first stage (the stage of reversal), because once that stage has been completed, the opposition no longer applies. Once the opposition has been deconstructed, "you don't need undecidability [or woman] any more" (195). He goes on to explain:

> There is one meaning to the word "woman" which is caught in the opposition, in the couple, and to this extent you can use the force of the woman to reverse, to undermine[,] this first stage of opposition. Once you have succeeded, the word "woman" does not have the same meaning. *Perhaps we could not speak of "woman" anymore.* (195; emphasis added)

This is the sort of reasoning that also accounts for his statement in "Choreographies" that the hymen no longer refers to the female body. Although Derrida may not speak of woman anymore, a feminist must continue to do so, and must go on, even, to speak of *women*. If feminists fail to reinstate the connection between woman and women, we will simply be repeating the displacement of woman from discourse. Irigaray, for example, returns to Plato and unearths the *chora* as the very matter, marked feminine, upon which Western philosophy has built itself as system. In the same way, a feminist reader of Derrida's texts, which similarly depend for their very functioning on woman's body, must insist on the existence of woman in the text. And, we must then go on to critically examine the function of woman in the text, and its function depends on its placing. As Spivak writes, "We cannot dismiss our double displacement by saying to ourselves: 'In the discourse of affirmative deconstruction, "we" are a "female element," which does not signify "female person"'" ("Displacement" 174). This is an instance where the connection between "woman" and "women" must be reinstated. Just as Derrida, out of necessity, insists that the hymen does not exist, so the feminist reader of Derrida must insist that whether actually or metaphorically, the hymen refers to the female body.

Irigaray's constant questioning of the sexualization of philo-

sophical and psychoanalytic discourse and of the way in which
these discourses try to pass themselves off as neutral is quite
revealing when one considers Derrida's metaphor of the hymen.
The subject—the producer of discourse—is always male, and the
object of his discourse is always based on the male subject, and
yet both subject and object are presented as universal. Consequently, Irigaray's argument continues, the other—woman—is
always suppressed and submitted to the economy of the same,
that is, the masculine. Another basic premise of Irigaray's readings is that phallogocentrism operates by exploiting the body-
matter of women and woman (*This Sex* 85), and it seems that
deconstruction may operate similarly. Although Derrida claims
that he resexualizes philosophical discourse with terms such as
the hymen, I have shown that he neutralizes it at the same time,
by insisting that his terms no longer refer in any way to the female
body. What happens if we take this would-be neutral discourse
and resexualize it? For if these terms no longer refer to the existential female body, they nevertheless refer to a textual construction of the female sexualized body and point to discourses where
this sexualized body is constructed. Derrida's terms have an
unmistakable signification in Freud's phallocentric theory of female
sexuality. The hymen functions there as a sign for the value of the
female as sexual commodity and the vagina functions there as a
hole, a "nothing-to-see" that signifies castration. The vagina is also
the privileged sexual organ to the exclusion of the clitoris and the
labia, organs that Irigaray privileges and reinscribes metaphorically in *This Sex Which Is Not One*, *An Ethics of Sexual Difference*,
and *Sexes and Genealogies*. Despite the fact that the hymen and invagination are reinscribed by Derrida as structural metaphors for
certain textual structures, they continue to point to the discourses
from which they come, perhaps implicating Derrida's text in the
systems of both psychoanalysis and metaphysics that his discourse
sets itself against. To insert Derrida's terms into the context of
psychoanalysis, or "into" the female body, may be to do a certain violence to them. But to do so is only to put them back into
the context from which they were initially and violently taken. To
do so is to resexualize them, in order to show that they cannot be
"desexualized" so easily and are therefore never neutral.

Mimesis: Configuring the Feminine in Irigaray

In an interview in *This Sex*, Irigaray has some cautionary remarks to make about the placing of woman in discourse. When asked about her desire to avoid a naive positioning of "the question of woman," Irigaray states that *Speculum* "is obviously not a book *about* woman; and it is still less . . . a 'studied gynecocentrism,' a 'place of the monopolization of the symbolic' to the benefit of a woman, or of some women" (*This Sex* 162). Like Derrida insisting that the hymen does not exist, Irigaray wants to avoid perpetuating the pitfalls of metaphysics; however, she does not eradicate the feminine from her discourse as Derrida does. What seems to be at stake here is asking the question of woman in a different way. She alludes to this again in another passage in *This Sex*: "[T]he issue is not one of elaborating a new theory of which woman would be the *subject* or *object*, but of jamming the theoretical machinery itself, of suspending its pretension to the production of a truth and of a meaning that are excessively univocal" (78). Where does the feminine enter into this project? The feminine, as represented in discourse, is the very means to this end of jamming the theoretical machinery. Elaborating on the way in which women should undertake to break down the production of theory, Irigaray writes:

> They should not put it, then, in the form "What is woman?" but rather, repeating/interpreting the way in which, within discourse, the feminine finds itself defined as lack, deficiency, or as imitation and negative image of the subject, they should signify that with respect to this logic a *disruptive excess* is possible on the feminine side. (78; emphasis in original)

What Irigaray describes here resembles the strategy she elsewhere names "mimesis" (76). Mimesis involves the deliberate donning of the traditional features of femininity: it is a "playful repetition," which brings to light "the cover-up of a possible operation of the feminine in language" (76). Once brought to light through mimesis, the feminine works as a disruptive force that is capable of upsetting the order and unity of phallogocentric discourse. For Irigaray, mimesis is an indirect and thus more effective response to the need to destroy "the discursive mechanism." Rather than the "direct feminist challenge" of "demanding to speak as a (masculine) 'subject'," which would only "maintain sexual indifference," Irigaray postulates the more subversive challenge of mimesis. Mimesis involves woman's acceptance of "'ideas,' in particular . . . ideas about herself that are elaborated in/by a masculine logic"; women take on these ideas with the aim of seeking out the way in which the feminine is exploited in discourse (76).

But if women mime the feminine, don't we risk simply being equated with those ideas about the feminine that we mime? For Irigaray, the answer is no: it is through performance, through assuming femininity as a role, that women signify the incommensurability of the feminine with "femininity" as it is elaborated within, for example, the discourse of psychoanalysis. Here, Irigaray's "mimesis" and Butler's "gender performance" have much in common. In other words, to assume femininity as a role signifies that femininity exceeds the "natural" traits that presumably correspond to the female sex. By the same token, femininity also exceeds any performance of femininity, an issue I will take up again in chapter 3 on *Nightwood* in my reading of Matthew O'Connor. On the subject of this excess of the feminine, Irigaray writes:

> [I]f women are such good mimics, it is because they are not simply resorbed in this function. *They also remain elsewhere:* another case of the persistence of "matter," but also of "sexual pleasure." (76; emphasis in original)

This passage points to the way in which "ideas about women" are capable of causing disruptions in discourse. The hymen in Derrida's writing works in this way, despite Derrida's intention to detach it from the woman's body. The association of woman with matter is partly what allows women to resist absorption into their mimed role. Matter, like sexual pleasure, is in itself excessive with respect to discourse. Since the terms "matter" and "sexual pleasure" are culturally marked as feminine, women, too, are excessive, or "remain elsewhere."[13] Mimesis is repetition with a difference, difference through repetition. Compared to gynesis, which consolidates the male subject in his displacement, the operation of mimesis makes visible the fact that masculine discourse is made possible through the exclusion of the feminine. Or, to invoke another concept of Irigaray's, phallogocentric discourse is founded on the eradication of woman, and mimesis brings this eradication to light.

Naomi Schor elaborates a typology of mimesis in order to distinguish between the generic feminist definition of the term and the radical definition of it in Irigaray's work. According to Schor, feminists interpret Irigarayan mimesis as "a parodic mode of discourse designed to deconstruct the discourse of misogyny through effects of amplification and rearticulation" (47). But Schor sees more radical implications in Irigaray's theory; she sees a more subversive version of mimesis that has been "largely misread, and even repressed" because it involves not a repudiation of misogyny but a reclamation of it (47). Schor describes Irigarayan mimesis as the "transvaluation" of misogynist discourse through the appropriation of misogynist terms: in other words, Irigarayan mimesis involves women identifying as their own those aspects of the feminine that have been used to oppress women (47).[14]

Schor is careful to describe precisely the relationship of the feminine to mimesis, focusing particularly on Irigaray's remark that mimesis makes " 'visible' . . . the cover-up of a possible operation of the feminine in language" (76). According to Schor, this more subversive type of mimesis will bring about "an emergence of the feminine" that "can only emerge from within or beneath . . . femininity, within which it lies buried" (48). "Femininity" here stands for the culturally constructed subject position of women and it covers up/makes invisible a more genuine aspect of woman, "the feminine." The metaphor of burial or repression seems to imply a feminine that exists prior to culture and discourse—in other words, an essential feminine. The point of Schor's article is to investigate those strands in Irigaray's writing that have led other feminists to label her writing essentialist, that is, writing that posits a natural, precultural femininity, rather than a contingent, cultural one. For Schor, Irigaray is not an essentialist; rather, her materialism has become confused with essentialism, which is often equated with biologism (50). The metaphor of a "buried" feminine that must be brought to light must not be simply equated with a feminine essence, because this buried feminine is conceived as part of the cultural construction of femininity and yet the buried feminine exceeds dominant representations of femininity. Schor describes the intricate connection of the subversive feminine with dominant femininity in this way:

> Irigaray's wager is that difference can be reinvented, that the bogus difference of misogyny can be reclaimed to become a radical new difference that would present the first serious historical threat to the hegemony of the male sex. Irigaray's wager is that there is a *(la/une femme)* woman *in* femininity. (47; emphasis in original)

As Schor clearly states here, the subversive, other feminine is neither before nor beyond femininity (the cultural construct); rather, it is *in* femininity. Thus, the subversive feminine is itself part of culture. By drawing attention to this subversive feminine, Irigaray writes the difference of the feminine, instead of rehearsing the familiar notion of the feminine as difference itself (the opposite of man). It is this notion of the subversive feminine that the models of displacement and mimesis share, strangely enough.

In Spivak's analysis of displacement, she contends that the reason Derrida takes woman as his model is woman's ability to dissimulate or impersonate—in other words, her capacity for masquerade (170, 177). According to Derrida in *Spurs*, it is "because she does not believe in the truth ... [that] woman remains a model ... She plays at dissimulation, at ornamentation, deceit, artifice, at an artist's philosophy" (67). The place of woman is ready-made for displacement because woman excels at impersonation and masquerade, that is, mimesis. Another way to say this is that woman's nonidentity makes her a perfect model for deconstructive discourse.[15] Derrida formulates woman's nonidentity in terms of woman's relation to distance: "[T]he <woman> is not a determinable identity ... Perhaps woman—a non-identity, a non-figure, a simulacrum—is distance's very chasm, the out-distancing of distance, the interval's cadence, distance itself, if we could still say such a thing, distance *itself*" (*Spurs* 49; emphasis in original). Derrida begins by describing woman in by now familiar terms ("a non-identity, a non-figure"), which build into increasingly inflated and repeated terms ("the out-distancing of distance . . . distance itself . . . distance *itself*"). Over the course of this passage, the distance between women and woman grows exponentially as Derrida allegorizes woman as "distance itself." Derrida's formulation of woman begins to sound strangely like Irigaray's, and if this is the case, Derrida's woman may mimetically undo his text.

In other words, if women remain always elsewhere in mimesis, as Irigaray writes, and women's capacity for mimicry is the reason they are displaced, then they also remain elsewhere in displacement.

> *Elsewhere of "matter":* if women can play with mimesis, it is because they are capable of bringing new nourishment to its operation. Because they have always nourished this operation? Is not the "first" stake in mimesis that of re-producing (from) nature? Of giving it form in order to appropriate it for oneself? As guardians of "nature," are not women the ones who maintain, thus who make possible, the resource of mimesis for men? (*This Sex* 76–77; emphasis in original)

Here Irigaray refers to the origins of the term mimesis as an imitation of nature, and suggests that women have a fundamental relation to this originary meaning. Women would then, it seems, have a fundamental role in the very operation of representation. But, once again, woman is in excess with respect to her relation to nature as well. Irigaray is careful to write that women are "*guardians* of 'nature'," not nature itself. In other words, this is a role that has been assigned to women, and they are not absorbed in this role either: they maintain a distance from it, just as they maintain a distance from any representation. But woman's nonidentity also allows her to resist appropriation, for it is this distance that makes her a good mimic. If we take this concept of woman and think of displacement in this light, the question arises, can there be appropriation if what is appropriated does not belong to woman, but is instead a mimed role? Does woman truly have "a place" that belongs to her and may be taken from her? If there is no property and no owner, how can we speak of appropriation or displacement? Is it contradictory to use the displacement model in order to critique masculine discourse and, at the same time, to use the mimesis model in order to show the subversive potential of the feminine, and the performative gender model to show that gender is constructed and not inherent, as I do throughout this study? Mimesis represents a bridge between displacement and performative gender. As such, mimesis is a way of maintaining a connection between feminist discourse and gender studies/queer studies. In the readings of the novels that follow, I trace vestiges of the notion of fundamental gender difference even in contexts where a decidedly performative model of gender seems to operate.[16] It is possible to argue that man cannot speak from the place of woman, as I do in my reading of *Nightwood*, and at the same time to argue that gender is never fixed, but constantly shifting, as I do in my reading of *The Talking Room*. The gender studies notion of the shifting, unstable nature of gender—in other words, the emphasis on performance or construction rather than on essence—is suggested in the work of Irigaray and Spivak that I discuss here. This similarity suggests continuity rather than a vast divide between this strain of feminism and gender studies. Woman's nonidentity— her distance from herself—makes her a desirable model for the deconstructive philosopher, for her place may be easily appropriated, and this notion of woman and identity informs the social constructivist account of gender as well. But woman's nonidentity is also the very thing that provides a tool for the feminist reader who wishes to read such a displacement, or, in general, to read against the grain of misogynist discourse. Displacement and mimesis have much in common because they are both symptoms of the lack of genuine sexual difference, and performative gender is a related symptom. Man needs woman to become a body; women mime femininity because femininity is but a reflection of masculine sameness. Irigaray's concept of the sensible transcendental, which is the focus of the last section of this chapter, is an attempt to overcome the divisions that are at the bottom of this problem.

Feminism and Gender Studies

What does feminist literary criticism stand to gain by focusing on gender construction and gender ambiguity in literary works? I bring together here the work of both feminist literary critics and theorists and the newer work of gender theorists, such as Judith Butler, in order to argue that these two disciplines must work together despite apparent conflicts. I will be staging a confrontation between feminist studies and gender studies by analyzing Tania Modleski's reading of Judith Butler. Modleski very clearly characterizes feminism and gender studies as divergent, but this position rests on a misreading of the aims of gender studies. Modleski views the advent of gender studies as an offshoot—or, in some cases, a replacement—of feminist studies. As a type of postfeminist criticism, gender studies operates on the assumption that feminism has succeeded in its aims, while at the same time it seeks to "undermin[e] the goals of feminism" (3). In Modleski's critique, Butler stands in not only for the whole field of gender studies but also for antiessentialist feminism (17–18). Modleski's main criticism is that Butler, as an antiessentialist, advocates "moving beyond gender" by means of gay camp parody, in other words, gender performance (157). Butler sees gender as consisting of "a relationship among sex, gender, sexual practice, and desire" (*Gender Trouble* 18). Gender is performative in the sense that it "constitut[es] the identity it is purported to be . . . There is no gender identity behind the expressions of gender; that identity is performatively constituted by the very 'expressions' that are said to be its results" (25). According to Modleski, drag, which brings to light the way in which gender is performative in Butler's analysis, is strangely "exempt from the rule" that "systems of revolutionary thought . . . are implicated in, and frequently the effect of, the systems they seek to undermine" (157). In other words, while Butler, as a good deconstructive theorist, finds even oppositional theoretical systems bound up with dominant systems of representation, she conceptualizes drag as a utopian possibility unconstrained by preexisting cultural practices. While Butler does indeed formulate drag as a subversive and therefore revolutionary possibility, drag is also, according to Butler, very much "implicated in" and "the effect of" the systems it seeks to "undermine," which are the binary gender system and the regime of compulsory heterosexuality. Far from signifying the possibility of "moving beyond gender," drag creates more genders, as it were, and it does so by taking up and redeploying the signs of the binary gender system, that is, the cultural markers of masculinity and femininity. In fact, it is precisely because drag works within our familiar gender scheme and then creates "dissonance" within it that it is potentially subversive.[17] Not only is it impossible to transcend gender, but to transcend a system is to leave it intact rather than to alter it.

To what degree is Modleski's argument that Butler advocates "moving beyond gender" valid? This is a common critique of the social constructivist theory of gender: Sandra Gilbert and Susan Gubar in *Sexchanges*, for example, fault this theory of gender for doing away with the gender of the author and treating it as irrelevant. Butler, however, repeatedly denounces the idea of a state beyond gender, as well as the related idea of a transcendence of any existing power structure. She writes, for example, that her text is

> an effort to think through the possibility of subverting and displacing those naturalized and reified notions of gender that support masculine hegemony and heterosexist power, to make gender trouble, not through the strategies that figure a *utopian beyond*, but through the mobilization, subversive confusion, and proliferation of precisely those constitutive categories that seek to keep gender in its place. (33–34; emphasis added)

Gender is troublesome because it displaces those categories—masculine and feminine—"that seek to keep gender in its place." The leap to the "utopian beyond" is finally not much of a threat, because it leaves systems of power behind, and, thus, intact. One of the essential points of Butler's work (and in this way she is a descendant of Irigaray and Derrida) is that subversion must come from within.

It is easy to understand Modleski's criticism that Butler is advocating the transcendence of gender, since Butler's language sometimes hints at this. But these hints are well qualified and Butler recognizes the impossibility, as well as the undesirability, of this sort of transcendence. Butler seems to invoke transcendence when writing of Monique Wittig's fictional characters who transgress conventional gender categories . Butler writes that these characters do not represent "a *transcendence* of the binary . . . The force of Wittig's fiction . . . is to offer an experience beyond the categories of identity, an erotic struggle to create new categories from the ruins of the old, new ways of being a body within the cultural field, and whole new languages of description" (127).[18] Butler seems both to deny the possibility of transcendence and to invoke it in this passage; yet careful reading shows that Butler describes this "experience *beyond* the categories of identity" as taking place firmly within culture, rather than beyond it. "New categories" are created, yet "from the ruins of the old"; "new ways of being a body" are also created, yet these are located "within the cultural field." And both of these new states are reached only through "struggle." In other words, there is no getting outside culture, or its systems of power, as many deconstructive theorists have noted before Butler. There is, however, a more desirable possibility: transforming culture and power from within. Butler sums up this issue within the specific field of gay and lesbian studies when she writes: "[T]he normative focus of gay and lesbian practice ought to be on the subversive and parodic redeployment of power rather than on the impossible fantasy of its full-scale transcendence" (124). It is clear that we are to understand gender acts as resignifications and realignments of the cultural constructs of masculinity and femininity and thus as cultural constructs themselves. Performative gender does not constitute a state "beyond gender" and hence beyond culture.

Butler neither denies gender nor does away with it as a category of analysis. Women are not irrelevant to Butler, as Modleski suggests. It is indeed possible and necessary to speak of women still; in fact, Butler's theoretical paradigms allow us to speak in a more complex fashion of women, that is, of the constructed nature of womanhood and femininity. To say that my gender is not something that I am, but something that I enact or do, is not to say that I am not a woman. Rather, it is to say that the way in which I am gendered is capable of change and modification, because gender is a process rather than a fixed state. Furthermore, gender studies allows us to see that the two expected answers to the question "What is my gender?" are not enough. What are the words to describe the multiple and discordant gender identities beyond masculine and feminine involving various combinations of sex, gender, sexual practice, and desire, the components of gender identity according to Butler? Our language isn't up to this task. Woolf's "other sexes" is one way of gesturing toward such complexity. Irigaray's concept of the sensible transcendental similarly points toward various possibilities for conceiving of difference anew.

Irigaray's Return to the Body

> In all his creations, all his works, man always seems to neglect thinking of himself as flesh, as one who has received his body as that primary home . . . which determines the possibility of his coming into the world. (Irigaray, *An Ethics* 127–28)

While man neglects thinking of himself as flesh, as body, woman cannot do so, because she is flesh, she is body, and, further, she gives the body/home to all beings (*An Ethics* 127). This is a fundamental principle of Irigaray's feminist philosophy, and I would argue, of the feminist fiction discussed in this book. Although Irigaray critiques the designation of the body as female, she also repeatedly stresses our origin in the maternal, female body, as she does here. The problem with the designation of the body as female is that this precludes the connection of woman with the intellectual, spiritual, and transcendental (and it also precludes the connection of man with body). The primary division of being is the division into mind and body, and the assignment of these categories, respectively, to masculine and feminine. And the primary division means that a genuine sexual difference does not exist (*An Ethics* 15). Irigaray's 1970s texts such as *This Sex* and *Speculum* reveal this dissociation between man and woman, soul and body, and related terms at work in the discourses of philosophy and psychoanalysis. She lays bare the ways in which these discourses construct themselves through a repudiation of the feminine and all that is associated with it: body, matter, and the senses. This repudiation of the feminine is revealed in part through the strategy of mimesis or masquerade, which leads to the privileging of the feminine. The first stage of Irigaray's overall project of conceiving of genuine sexual difference involves uncovering the feminine in its specificity, and mimesis is one of the key means to retrieving the feminine from its place as the reflection of masculine sameness. Once this dissociation, or "severing," of masculine and feminine is uncovered, the next step is to restore the broken tie. Irigaray's approach to this restoration takes somewhat different forms in the earlier and later texts, but these approaches are all related to the female body. In "When Our Lips Speak Together" from *This Sex,* she envisions an ideal love between women as the means of overcoming this breach. In later texts such as *An Ethics of Sexual Difference* and *Sexes and Genealogies,* however, it is heterosexual love that allows for the empirical development of sexual difference and the concept of the sensible transcendental that allows for the transcendental development of sexual difference.[19] While Irigaray argues for an exclusively heterosexual love as a means of healing the breach between masculine and feminine, I argue that this is too narrow a basis for a full flowering of difference. Models of sexual difference that are based in heterosexual models, like Irigaray's, reaffirm binary and hierarchical notions of gender, a problem that Irigaray herself points out when she calls for a nonhierarchical model of sexual difference (*An Ethics* 110).[20] Irigaray herself leaves room for such a reading when she writes of the heterosexual encounter involving "wonder" (82). The encounter between man and woman is a reflection of the encounter between "the most material and the most metaphysical," that is, the sensible transcendental, which involves "A third dimension . . . Neither the one nor the other. Which is not to say neutral or neuter" (82). That is, we must think outside of one of the fundamental binaries—the sex/gender binary. In fact, wonder cannot, strictly speaking, be thought within the framework of difference as we know it. For this reason, wonder may come about in the same-sex encounter just as much as it does in the heterosexual encounter, an issue I explore in more detail in chapter 5 on *Written on the Body.*

This meeting of opposed concepts takes several forms in Irigaray's writing, as well as in the novels by Woolf, Barnes, Hauser, and Winterson that are my subject here. Irigaray fleshes out her concept of the sensible transcendental variously through the figures of the angel, the mucus, the double lips of the female body, and the sexual encounter.[21] Each of these feminine figures is related to the sensible transcendental because it involves the crossing of boundaries and is a third term that subverts the gender binary. Irigaray's concept of the sensible transcendental closely resembles many figures that appear in my text: Woolf's little language, Barnes's third sex, Hauser's secret second tongue, and Winterson's bodily writing. These figures serve as ways to see past the line that demarcates the division of concepts—the line that separates and subordinates one term of a binary opposition from the other. In this sense, they stand for the reintegration of oppositions, which in the case of sex/gender, come together in the form of "other sexes." Like Woolf, Irigaray opens up possibilities by pointing to a realm of sexual difference beyond the one we know.

TWO

"THIS DIFFERENCE . . . THIS IDENTITY . . . WAS OVERCOME"
Reintegrating Masculine and Feminine in Virginia Woolf's The Waves

The subject as a self-identical entity is no more.
—Judith Butler, *Bodies That Matter*

As Bernard, the figure of the writer in Virginia Woolf's *The Waves*, begins his "summing up," his story of stories, he describes the limitations of narrative and his longing for another mode of expression.

> How tired I am of stories, how tired I am of phrases that come down beautifully with all their feet on the ground! Also, how I distrust neat designs of life that are drawn upon half sheets of notepaper. I begin to long for some little language such as lovers use, broken words, inarticulate words, like the shuffling of feet on the pavement. (Woolf, *The Waves* 238)

Losing both his faith and his interest in stories, with which he is identified from the beginning of the novel, Bernard turns to the "little language" as a more genuine means of expression. Bernard's desire for "some little language" in place of "neat designs of life" is one of the key issues of the text—the struggle between a fragmentary, feminine language of the body and a narrative, masculine language of the mind. Bernard is able to connect these two types of languages—in effect, he learns to speak both ways—and I focus on this process, for by means of this reconnection, Woolf effects a healing of the classic split between masculine and feminine that structures Western thought.

While the feminine little language represents what is so fragmentary and fundamental that it is nearly nonlinguistic, the masculine

narrative language represents those order and logic-making processes of abstraction that try to tame the nearly nonlinguistic.[1]
Consequently, the stakes of this opposition between a feminine
language and a masculine language and of the eventual overcoming of this opposition are high indeed: Woolf seeks to reintegrate
the degraded, repudiated feminine, here represented by a certain
type of language, with the privileged and the central, that is to
say, the masculine.[2] This central aspect of Woolf's fictional text
seems inspired by the same aims as certain theoretical texts of
Irigaray, which also call for a restoration of the feminine and a
healing of the split between masculine and feminine, a fictional/
theoretical connection that I explore throughout this study.
Through the reconnection of these oppositionally defined languages,
Woolf's text achieves a series of other reconnections: the barriers
between form/formlessness, mind/body, intellect/sensation, and
identity/nonidentity are crossed over. Rather than privileging one
term at the expense of the other, Woolf attempts to integrate concepts and to see beyond opposition. The reunion of languages and
identities is particularly closely related. In Woolf's view, language
is so fundamental to the construction of identity that to learn to
speak both a masculine and a feminine language is also to learn to
be both masculine and feminine. For Woolf, the relation between
language and subjectivity is at least double. Although subjects
are constructed in and through language, it is precisely the unstable,
slippery nature of language that works to undo subjectivity. Again,
Woolf sees beyond opposition, taking what is defined as different
and fundamentally opposed and showing its interrelation: identity is implicated in nonidentity; masculinity is implicated in femininity. But the interrelation of these terms is only achieved through
struggle and debate. In fact, the text endlessly questions the problems of identity. The six friends engage in their most extended
meditations on identity and anonymity at their two meetings, the
going-away party for Percival in section 4 and the reunion dinner
at Hampton Court in section 8.[3]

The Waves interrogates the construction of identity through
both Rhoda and Bernard, whose grapplings with the subject are
the most far-reaching. Bernard and Rhoda best exemplify the tension between identity and nonidentity in the novel: early in the
novel, Bernard represents the individual who clings to identity

and Rhoda represents the individual who is unable to claim any identity at all.[4] Yet, these two characters only seem to be positioned at opposite ends of the spectrum with regard to identity. Rhoda is presented as in crisis from the start, while Bernard's crisis develops and builds throughout the novel. Rhoda, who "has no face," stands for the feminine precluded from entry into the symbolic, while Bernard at times exemplifies the masculine subject, embedded in discourse and commanding his subjectivity. Yet, at other times, Bernard experiences self-fragmentation to a high degree and these experiences build in intensity over the course of the novel. Rhoda represents for Bernard the state that he longs to attain—a state of dissolved and dissipated identity that he finds more authentic than a well-defined identity. Like a contemporary post-structuralist theorist, Bernard seeks to dismantle his subjectivity and, thus, he takes woman as his figure/model in a displacement of the feminine in Spivak's sense. Bernard's "text" might also be said to be a gynetic one in Jardine's sense: in it, feminine non-identity is privileged and this privileging is a key to the text's modernity. But for Rhoda, this state of nonidentity causes anguish and pain and eventually leads to her suicide. When Rhoda is thus written out of the text, Bernard's path to nonidentity is cleared: he is only able to divest himself of his identity by taking the figure of woman as his model. Rhoda's death enables his own transformation into a "man without a self." Despite the similarity of this exchange to displacement, in this process the feminine is not completely eradicated or appropriated. Rhoda is written out of the text, but the feminine that she stands for is preserved in the form of several figures of women that emerge as Bernard makes his transformation to a state of gender fluidity.

"Finding Sequences Everywhere": Stories and the Construction of Masculine Identity

Writing about the critical reception of The Waves in her diary, Woolf remarked that it was "[o]dd that they (The Times) shd. praise my characters when I meant to have none" (Diary 4: 47). We should take her statement to mean that the concept of character is meaningless in a text that shows stable identity to be a fiction.

"Character," the unified representation of a person in a piece of literature, relies on the idea of a unified self or identity that can be re-presented. Critics of the novel retain this traditional concept of character when they argue that Bernard and his friends are not in fact six distinct characters, but rather a united whole, since a union of characters still implies one large overall character.[5] In *The Waves*, this concept of character, and the concept of unified selfhood on which it is based, is questioned through the privileging of decentered, marginalized subjectivity such as Rhoda's and Bernard's. Despite Woolf's warning about character, I will focus a great deal on character as well, for by means of her (non)characters Woolf questions the notion of a unified self.

One of the main themes of the novel is the growth of the six characters, particularly the development of their consciousnesses, as many critics have noted.[6] Yet the emphasis on the growth of the individual and the corresponding chronological, teleological frame of the novel (first words to last words, sunrise to sunset, birth to death) form only one side of the picture. While the building up of identity goes on, identity is, at the same time, being relentlessly questioned and undercut through the structure of identity itself, that is, its foundation in language, which brings about its dissipation or disintegration. These two functions of language in relation to identity are also, not surprisingly, gendered. Identity is shown to be made (and repeatedly remade) in and through narrative, masculine language, while it is unmade through fragmentary, feminine language. It is this process that I will focus on here, for I feel that part of what is radical in Woolf's novelistic practice is her method of making novels out of the opposite of the presumably novelistic: anonymity rather than identity, silence rather than speech, monologue rather than dialogue, solitude rather than society, the isolated moment rather than moments strung together.[7]

While Rhoda is disdainful of identity, Bernard revels in being "Bernard"; Rhoda's anguish over identity in the early sections of the novel is matched by Bernard's easy assumption of identity. Bernard bases his belief in the possibility of identity on his idea of sequence. As a child, Bernard tells us that he sees sequences everywhere, and this is what makes him a storyteller (132–33). Sequence is the marker of stories for Bernard; it makes a story a story. Sequence also forms the link between clear-cut identity and the masculine language of stories: Bernard finds his identity confirmed by the same images of sequential movement that form the basis of stories. In fact, Bernard feels that, without the linked words of stories, he is "in darkness . . . [is] nothing" (132–33).

For Bernard, stories have a magical power of restoring his belief in the order of life, and yet this sense of order is undercut in the novel. As soon as he is able to perceive consecutive movement in the world, he is able to recover from the most profound doubts about stories. In the following passage, the middle-aged Bernard begins to feel that his old habit of making up stories about the people he sees is so arbitrary that it is an "imposition" on what is real: "But why impose my arbitrary design? Why stress this and shape that and twist up little figures like the toys men sell in trays in the street? Why select this, out of all that,—one detail?" (188). But Bernard's confidence in the viability of stories is soon restored when he suddenly feels the world falling back into order, which is to say, when events appear to be sequential: this allows him to become a part of the world once again. Bernard soon gets swept up in the sequence that keeps the world in motion.

> But observe how dots and dashes are beginning, as I walk, to run themselves into continuous lines . . . The world is beginning to move past me like the banks of a hedge when the train starts, like the waves of the sea when a steamer moves. *I am moving too, am becoming involved in the general sequence when one thing follows another* and it seems inevitable that the tree should come, then the telegraph-pole, then the break in the hedge. And as I move, surrounded, included and taking part, the usual phrases begin to bubble up . . . (188; emphasis added)

Here, Bernard's phrasemaking, which relies on sequence for shape and form, is prompted by "the general sequence" that he perceives in the world around him.[8] But the question remains whether there is sequence in the world or whether sequence is merely in the eye of the perceiver: Rhoda sees meaningless chaos in the same world in which Bernard sees meaningful order. Moreover, in this and other passages where Bernard finds reassurance in the world for his doubts in the continuity of either stories or identity, the order in the world is man-made and imposed; it is not part of the natural order of things. Following Bernard's own metaphors in the passage, it is the train's movement or the steamer's movement past natural objects that gives him his sense of order. The phenomenal world for Woolf is full of disorder and destruction: it is only through human constructions, whether of identity, story, or locomotion, that the natural world is shaped and formed.

As he ages, Bernard not only begins to find sequence or narrative impossible but also undesirable. Linear stories are reductive: they force disparate sensations and experiences into a neat package, thereby doing violence to their individual parts. Fragmentary language, on the other hand, which is privileged under the name of the "little language," allows discrete sensations to remain discrete; it forces no order or progressive movement upon them.[9] At the end of the novel, the association of sequence with the masculine language of stories is altered greatly when Bernard brings together fragment and story, masculine and feminine languages. As Bernard grows older, his phrases have the tendency to resemble fragments more and more: no longer linked, the phrases stand apart as discrete units. The reason for the change is that Bernard's sense of the fragment grows, while his belief in the possibility of imposing order on "incoherence" diminishes. In the same way, his sense of the instability and fragmentation of identity grows, while his faith in the stability and wholeness of identity dissipates. As Bernard thus begins to realize the inadequacy of stories, he attributes this to their failure to follow an orderly sequence. Bernard also dwells on the necessity of sequence in life, but at the same time he comes to realize that it is a necessary fiction. Rather than reject sequence outright, the novel suggests that sequence is needed in order to keep disorder and nothingness at bay, both in stories and in life itself.

"I Have No Face": Femininity and Nonidentity

Rhoda is unable to claim or construct an identity for herself: although she feels disgust for the false trappings of identity, she also longs to be able to present herself simply, as she imagines Jinny and Susan do. When alone, Rhoda can ignore the pressure of "the individual life" (105), but among other people, she feels, "I am broken into separate pieces; I am no longer one" (106). At the reunion dinner of the six friends at Hampton Court, Rhoda remarks with disgust that in their presence she "must go through the antics of the individual" (224); that is, she must acknowledge their claims to individuality, "your children, your poems, your chilblains or whatever it is that you do and suffer" (224). Her derision for the markers of identity—she places children and poems alongside of chilblains—could not be more clear. Rhoda is very lucid about the striking difference between herself and her friends in terms of their attachment to identity. Arriving at Hampton Court, she remarks: "I perceived, from your coats and umbrellas, even at a distance, how you stand embedded in a substance made of repeated moments run together; are committed, have an attitude, with children, authority, fame, love, society; where I have nothing. I have no face" (222–23). Rhoda's statement "I have no face" sums up her anonymous state: she lacks the fundamental marker of identity.[10] Rhoda's friends often identify her by her very lack of identity; just as Bernard is identified as the storyteller, Rhoda is identified as the anonymous one who shrinks from society. Although Rhoda exemplifies this state of extreme anonymity in the novel, the desire to shed markers of identity and to become blurred and faceless is a desire shared by every character of The Waves at one point or another. This is anticipated by Rhoda, who notes that again and again she must endure the moment when "Identity failed me" because of her realization that "We are nothing" (64).[11] The other characters maintain some belief in the notion that "we are something," but they soon become aware of the condition that Rhoda has taken for granted since childhood.

Rhoda is alienated from the body to the same degree to which Susan and Jinny are identified with it. In order to "call [her]self back to the body" (44), Rhoda requires the shock of physical sensation. Unlike her friends, Rhoda is not rooted in her body; thus, she cannot speak the direct language of the "voice of action" as they do, because she lacks the clear-cut and precise identity that they enjoy. And yet, Rhoda does not speak the indirect, abstract language of the men. Rhoda's lack of a clear-cut identity places her in a privileged position for examining the nature of language, because for Woolf, egotism, such as Bernard possesses, blocks a genuine understanding of the nature of language. Bernard is only able to arrive at the same conclusions that Rhoda has when he becomes a "man without a self" in his summing up.

The meeting at Hampton Court is a turning point in the novel's reflections on identity: at this point, identity becomes an issue fraught with difficulty for all the characters, not only Rhoda. They now want to shed one identity and create another, while at the same time realizing the need for identity. The group once again brings out not only the tendency toward union but also the insistent assertion of individuality, so that each character, as Neville remarks, must show his or her "credentials," or claims to identity. For Rhoda, these assertions of individual identity are not only impossible but also undesirable because they are inherently violent, and, for this reason, she must escape from them. Rhoda calls these claims to attention "pluckings and searchings" (224) that have no real impact on her. She also knows that social intercourse, which she derides as "the antics of the individual," is finally meaningless: "After all these callings hither and thither, these pluckings and searchings, I shall fall alone through this thin sheet into gulfs of fire. And you will not help me." Rather than finding the ability to create an identity reassuring, as she did with Jinny and Susan at Percival's party, Rhoda now finds it meaningless because of her sense of radical alienation and solitude. But Rhoda also envisions an escape from identity and worldliness in an act of the imagination: "I could fancy that we might blow so vast a bubble that the sun might set and rise in it and we might . . . be cast off and escape from here and now" (224). Rhoda's "bubble" might be a story, like Bernard's air ball of childhood, or it might be the self-enclosed world of *The Waves* in which the sun does indeed "set and rise." This section closes on a strong image of anonymity, which is an answer to Rhoda's desire to escape from the need for identity in the "here and now." This image also helps to ease the pressure that the group has brought to bear on each individual to form an identity in the presence of others.

As the section at Hampton Court draws to a close, the clearest affirmation of anonymity and androgyny over identity and clear-cut gender takes place. Louis and Rhoda have a vision of draped figures of ambiguous gender emerging from the sea. "There are figures coming towards us. Are they men or are they women? They still wear the ambiguous draperies of the flowing tide in which they have been immersed" (231). This tide, which Louis has just identified as "life" ("Life tumbles its catch upon the grass" [231]), has draped them in clothes that disguise gender: here, the tide represents the unity brought about by the dissipation of identity that the characters have sought in each of their meetings. The figures come nearer, and Rhoda is disappointed when gender and identity are once again distinguishable:

> Now . . . as they pass that tree, they regain their natural size. They are only men, only women. Wonder and awe change as they put off the draperies of the flowing tide . . . Now light falls on them again. They have faces. They become Susan and Bernard, Jinny and Neville, people we know. Now what a shrinkage takes place! Now what a shrivelling, what an humiliation! (231–32)

Before, as anonymous figures with questionable gender (for they are neither androgynous nor neuter), they caused "wonder" and "awe" in Rhoda, but now that they are clearly men and women with recognizable faces, they repel her ("what a shrinkage . . . what a shrivelling," she thinks as she sees them). Rhoda prizes anonymity and ambiguity because they allow for multiplicity, diversity, and difference—that is, a wide range, rather than a limited set, of possibilities. Once these figures resume their identities, Rhoda reacts violently to them, feeling as she always does the shock of identity: "The old shivers run through me, hatred and terror, as I feel myself grappled to one spot by these hooks they cast on us; these greetings, recognitions" (232).

Louis, who has always wanted his friends to unite into one whole, is also critical of the resumption of identity by his friends. As they break into the solitude he shared with Rhoda, he remarks that he and Rhoda are forced to reestablish their identities:

> Who are you? Who am I? . . . the eye brightens and all the insanity of personal existence without which life would fall flat and die, begins again. They are on us . . . we push off in to the tide of the violent and cruel sea. *Lord help us to act our parts* as we greet them returning—Susan and Bernard, Neville and Jinny. (232; emphasis added)

Although Louis's disgust for the abrupt return to identity is clear from his remark about "the insanity of personal existence," his acknowledgment of its necessity and unavoidability is clear when he qualifies it with the phrase, "without which life would fall flat and die." His "prayer," "Lord help us to act our parts as we greet them returning," suggests once again that identity is not a set of inherent traits but an act or a role that we must perform. Louis's image of "the tide of the violent and cruel sea" suggests the pulsing of extreme emotion that he always associates with the return of individuality. But the figures initially emerged from "the flowing tide": the waves signify both the matter in which false identity is dissolved—the blurring of distinctions—as well as the insistent, inescapable need for individual identity, which is a need for distinctions.[12] This double nature of identity marks Bernard's struggles with it, struggles that he is only able to resolve through incorporating into his own identity the figure of Rhoda, who has brought these issues to the fore.

Rhoda represents Woolf's conception of the modern subject: it is composed of parts that do not form a whole; its conscious mind is divided by the forces of the unconscious; and it is self-conscious enough to be aware of these qualities.[13] That is, the modern subject not only lacks a stable and unified identity, which is the basis of the premodern subject, but also has extreme doubts about the very possibility of such a thing. At the same time that Woolf creates a notion of displaced subjectivity in Rhoda, she also creates a notion of stable and unified identity in Susan and Jinny, one that is formed through a connection to the body and the material world, rather than to the mind and the intellect. It is important to note that Woolf complicates her notion of gendered identity and gendered relationships to language to a great degree. While Rhoda shares certain traits with Susan and Jinny, she also diverges widely from them. The only other character who comes close to Susan and Jinny in his or her relation to the body is Percival, a man. Among the other men, Bernard and Louis exemplify a traditionally masculine identity and relationship to language that are based on the principles of self-identity and sameness; yet Bernard becomes more and more like Neville and Rhoda over the course of the novel, and even Louis is associated with Rhoda in many respects. Woolf's modernism places her in the midst of such a struggle, one that is marked by nostalgia for the old forms of the past and yearning for the new forms of the future.

The Feminine "Little Language"

At the farewell party for Percival, Louis is the first to identify a certain type of language as a "little language." The "little language" erupts when the connection uniting the six friends has broken and they return to individual identity. When the circle of common experience breaks, they return to the stream of life, which is filled with emotion and action. The "voice of action" is described here as the response to the call of desire:

> Listen, Rhoda . . . to *the casual, quick, exciting voice of action*, of hounds running on the scent. *They speak now without troubling to finish their sentences. They talk a little language such as lovers use.* An imperious brute possesses them. The nerves thrill in their thighs. Their hearts pound and churn in their sides. Susan screws her pocket-handkerchief. Jinny's eyes dance with fire. (142–43; emphasis added)

The voice of action, prompted by desire—the "imperious brute"—is like the call of the hunt, suggested by the phrase "hounds running on the scent." Because of the intensity of their desire ("their hearts pound and churn"), the lovers speak in short phrases or fragments (their speech is "casual, quick, exciting").[14] While the masculine language of stories is often associated with writing (e.g., Bernard's habit of committing his thoughts to his "book of phrases"), the feminine "little language" is always spoken. The speakers do not need to complete their sentences, because the "little language" is readily understandable; immediacy is its key. Louis specifically mentions Jinny and Susan in connection with this language of desire, Jinny because of her association with the body and sexuality, and Susan because of her connection with the earth and mothering. Just as Rhoda's anonymity provides the model for Bernard's gradual shedding of his identity, so Jinny's and Susan's "little language" provides the model for a closer connection to the world through language for all of the other characters.[15]

The "little language" has its foundation in the body, rather than the mind. In a passage in which Jinny describes her experience of speaking, she conceives of language as a physical act with physical aims, rather than as a mental act with mental aims, as we commonly perceive it:

> This is rapture; this is relief. The bar at the back of my throat lowers itself. Words crowd and cluster and push forth one on top of another. It does not matter which. They jostle and mount on each other's shoulders. The single and the solitary mate, tumble and become many. It does not matter what I say. Crowding, like a fluttering bird, one sentence crosses the empty space between us. It settles on his lips. (104)

Jinny's speech both relieves her desire ("This is rapture; this is relief") and indicates her desire in order to win its object. The result of this one exchanged sentence is her admission "to the warmth and privacy of another soul" (104). The physical nature of Jinny's experience of speaking extends to her perception of the words themselves, not just to her delivery of them. She describes the individual words emerging from her throat as having the shape and form of bodies ("They jostle and mount on each other's shoulders"). She is disdainful of both hierarchy and singularity: single words do not remain single, but "mate, tumble and become many."[16] For Jinny, "it does not matter which" word ends up on top or comes out first, for this is not a competition. Jinny's description of her language resembles the descriptions of feminine writing in the work of Luce Irigaray and Hélène Cixous: it is multiple, material, and immediate. There is also a direct correspondence between what Jinny's words say and what they do: her words "mate" and "tumble," just as the aim of Jinny's statement to the man at the party is to bring their bodies together, to close the space between them.

Jinny's connection to the body is so strong and direct that she does not need the mediating function of language in order to communicate. To describe her relation to her body as a "connection" is actually misleading, for "Jinny *is* her body," as Mark Hussey has noted: she lives her body in a way that is difficult to imagine, given Western culture's pervasive mind/body dualism.[17] She describes

the workings of "the body's imagination" as involving a perception of sensory objects without any sort of processing or abstraction of these perceptions. Jinny sees "things in outline. I see rocks
in bright sunshine. I cannot take these facts into some cave and,
shading my eyes, grade their yellows, blues, umbers into some
substance" (176). Jinny perceives the rocks, but is unable to retreat
into the mind, figured here as "some cave," where she would evalu-
ate and grade the rocks' colors by means of analysis. Rather, she
moves quickly from one sense perception to the next. Jinny claims
that she is unable to analyze what she perceives in order to make
subtle distinctions. Yet she is indeed making careful distinctions
among the colors when she notes the "yellows, blues, umbers";
the painterly "umber" especially indicates discernment and distinction. This contradiction between Jinny's claim about her language and her actual language raises a crucial question about
whether Jinny and Susan are in fact cut off from discursive language in practice, although they may be cut off from it in prevailing theories of feminine subjectivity and in their own perceptions.

As is clear from Jinny's description of her speech, a knowledge
of the "little language" is only possible through an intensification
of bodily sensations, which she, Susan, and Percival possess.[18]
Susan feels no gap between herself and what is around her; in
fact, she feels that she *is* the things around her: "I think I am the
field, I am the barn, I am the trees . . . I cannot be divided or kept
apart" (97). The "little language" connects people to the phenomenal world, while talk and stories divide people from it. Because
Susan "cannot be divided or kept apart," she feels that she is unable to command the distance and the objectivity needed to tell or
to understand a story. At this early stage in the novel, Susan represents the marginal position of the feminine in relation to symbolic
discourse and is often contrasted with Bernard, who represents
the subject fully embedded in the symbolic. These positions are
represented by Susan's claim that she is unable to make phrases
by stringing together words in a pattern, which is Bernard's fundamental activity. An exchange between Bernard and Susan as
children makes her perception of their differences clear.

Susan compares Bernard's great facility with language to her
inability to make more than a simple statement. Bernard remarks
that "we melt into each other with phrases," while Susan can only

make individual statements that neither merge with each other nor allow her to "melt into" another person: "'I see the beetle,' said Susan. 'It is black, I see; it is green, I see; I am tied down with single words. But you wander off; you slip away; you rise up higher, with words and words in phrases'" (16).[19] Susan feels that her relationship to language is the result of a failure to understand talk. Referring to Bernard, she says, "[I]t kills me when the object of my love shows by a phrase that he can escape. He escapes, and I am left clutching at a string that slips in and out among the leaves on the tree-tops. I do not understand phrases" (132). Here we see the conventional division between the feminine subject and the masculine subject in terms of their respective relationships to language. Bernard understands and creates phrases (the balloon on a string is a metaphor for his stories throughout the novel), while Susan understands only "cries of love, hate, rage and pain" and silence, as she self-consciously remarks (131). Yet despite her insistence that she is unable to tie words together, to tell a story, Susan's speech shows that she *does* in fact control language in this way: she is, after all, telling a story (about her inability to tell a story). Like Jinny, Susan self-consciously manipulates language to describe her frustration with her use of language. By engaging in this self-analysis, both women demonstrate that they do "understand phrases"; moreover, they are quite skilled at creating them. It is only Percival who lives in a completely unmediated and, therefore, silent relationship to the world.

Yet, despite her facility with language, Susan is convinced that her language, as she says, "ties her down," while Bernard's, on the other hand, frees him (he "wander[s] off" and "escapes" by means of his language). Susan, like the other characters in the novel, has accepted the cultural differences between masculinity and femininity as intrinsic differences, although her own speech and behavior show them to be conventions or constructions. Woolf continually shows her characters pushing against the constraints imposed by culturally determined gender differences, and these differences are revealed as constructs by means of Bernard's transformation into a fluidly gendered character who reunites masculine and feminine languages and subject positions by the end of the novel. Susan's envy of the masculine language is apparent, but she is also critical of this distanced, analytic language. Susan explains her preference for emotional expression and silence and her disgust with analytic language in response to the ceaseless analysis of her five friends as they meet to send Percival off to India. The masculine language, or "talk," is figured as a violent exposure of a woman's body: "The only sayings I understand are cries of love, hate, rage and pain. This talking is undressing an old woman whose dress had seemed to be part of her, but now, as we talk, she turns pinkish underneath, and has wrinkled thighs and sagging breasts. When you are silent you are again beautiful" (131). Susan distinguishes between three kinds of language here: "cries," which express fundamental emotions; "talk," which is likened to the violent undressing of an old woman; and "silence," which is the absence of language. When the old woman's dress, which had formerly been a "part of her," is taken off, her aging thighs and breasts are exposed to the eye and appear "wrinkled" and "sagging." Susan does not see the woman's body as ugly; rather, what is ugly by implication is talking itself, or disrobing and undressing through description and explanation. It is significant that the violence of talk is aimed at an old woman and that this talk exposes and violates her. Susan's metaphor implies that the violence of discourse and stories is aimed at women in particular. This violence is also textual in that the masculine language of talk or symbolic discourse functions by excluding or suppressing feminine language. Susan privileges silence over cries when she states that silence makes her addressee beautiful once again. Her addressee is her friends as a group who engage in talk about themselves, reveling in their identities, possessions, and jobs, all things that are alien to Susan, much as they are alien to Rhoda. In comparison to her friends, the people whom Susan admires are marked not by what they say but by what they do in silence: "I like to be with people who twist herbs, and spit into the fire and shuffle down long passages in slippers like my father" (131). Susan condemns not speech as such but the habit of talk when it is not necessary. She believes that language should *do* things—that it should perform a function such as expressing strong emotions, like the little language does, not just be produced for the sake of its production, as is the case with many of the characters' monologues in the novel.

Woolf uses Susan's analysis of the differences between talk, cries, and silence in order to introduce the main tension between masculine and feminine languages in the novel. This tension arises from constructed differences, not inherent ones. While masculine and feminine are opposed, they are only opposed initially: the entire narrative moves toward the reconnection of the two. This is clear when Bernard's experiences in his "summing up" (his greatest attempt at a teleological narrative) make him understand the need for the feminine "little language." There, Bernard adopts the feminine "little language" and joins it with his stories. Although the novel sets out to show that stories are imperfect because of what they exclude, as Susan demonstrates, it does not reject stories, for they prove to be not only inescapable but necessary, imperfect though they may be. Susan herself longs for the ability to tell stories, just as Bernard longs for the ability to speak the "little language."[20]

Jinny and Susan may seem to be barred from entry into the symbolic, and therefore cut off from language, but they use language with the same degree of analytic distance and skill that the male characters use. In this way, Woolf re-creates certain conventional gender differences with the aim of showing their eventual reunion, which takes place in Bernard's meditations on identity and language in his summing up, Neville's meditations on speech, writing, and poetry, and Rhoda's meditations on gaining access to the world through language. In each case, the characters struggle with oppositionally defined languages that are eventually conjoined in an overcoming of opposition.

Although Jinny and Susan are synonymous with the "little language," they are able to speak *about* their difficulty with sequence, stories, and analysis, and this self-criticism is itself, of course, a kind of analysis. They are also able to gain enough distance to describe the "little language": in effect, they tell stories about their use of language. In other words, they are acutely aware of their inability to speak like the men, but this very awareness should be impossible because of their supposed immersion in the world of concrete things, and their alienation from the symbolic order that this would indicate. By the same token, Bernard's status as a masculine subject, fully constituted in the symbolic, would seem to preclude the possibility of his desire for an immediate language of the body, but it does not. By showing these characters straining at the conventional gender distinctions with which they are identified, the novel suggests that the borders between a feminine language and a masculine language, between what is usually thought to be the "presymbolic" and the symbolic, are fluid and flexible. In this way, the novel avoids the essentializing implicit in a strict separation between the two. What Woolf is doing is locating something like a Kristevan semiotic, prediscursive realm (the monosyllabic "little language") *within* discourse and culture. It is not a realm below or outside culture, which would mean that the subversive possibilities of this other language are only temporary, and thus subordinate to the hegemony of the symbolic. At certain moments, the novel does locate the forces that disintegrate identity, as well as those that fragment sequential narrative, "beneath" or beyond life (e.g., Bernard's various experiences of self-loss and Louis's images of the eruption of the "little language" from beneath the stream of life). This may seem to indicate that these subversive forces emerge from a prediscursive realm, but in Jinny's and Susan's actual use of language, and in Bernard's remark that language is a stream made up of both stories and fragments (282), the "little language" is seen to be part of discourse itself. In the next section, I will pursue this connection between the "little language" and stories by examining Bernard's growing desire for "a howl; a cry" (295) and "a bark, a groan" (251). He longs for Susan's "cries of love, hate, rage and pain" (131) as a way to rescue his failed story of stories, his summing up. What happens to the coding of the "little language" as feminine when it is used by the masculine subject? Is this act best described as a violent appropriation or a peaceful reunion or some state in-between?

"Little Bits of Ourselves are Crumbling": Bernard's Deconstruction of Identity

The meeting of the friends at Hampton Court is a major turning point in Bernard's thinking about identity.[21] In this section, as I discussed above in relation to Rhoda, the friends reflect on their tendency to assert their individuality when they meet. It is this reliance upon the trappings of identity that prevents them from easily merging as a group. In Bernard's case, silence, or the absence of language, begins to clear a space for their union. Bernard describes

the effect of silence on his sense of identity: "As silence falls I am
dissolved utterly and become featureless and scarcely to be distinguished from another" (224). The fact that this loss of identity
is brought on by silence implies that language is what keeps nothingness at bay, creating the illusion (or reality) that there is life.
But "I" here must be read not just as referring to Bernard but as
the "I," or the first-person pronoun: the "I," the subject articulated
in language, also dissolves utterly through the effect of silence.
Yet if silence dissolves us, renders us anonymous, language is what
makes us have an identity in the first place. Language reinstates
identity after every lapse into anonymity in *The Waves*: at Percival's
farewell party, Bernard becomes an "I" by becoming an "eye," an
observer or storyteller. But before Bernard manages to restore his
sense of identity, he remarks on the feeling of loss: "[W]e are slipping away. Little bits of ourselves are crumbling. There! Something very important fell then. I cannot keep myself together" (235).
This experience of self-fragmentation at Hampton Court is so profound that Bernard retells it in his "summing up," for in that final
section of the novel he finally becomes "a man without a self," a
transformation that is made possible by these repeated experiences
of self-loss.

Bernard's gloss, or "summing up," of this experience turns on
an image of water:

> *I could not collect myself; I could not distinguish myself;* I could not
> help letting fall the things that had made me a minute ago eager,
> amused, jealous, vigilant and hosts of other things into the wa-
> ter. *I could not recover myself from that endless throwing away, dissi-*
> *pation, flooding forth without our willing it* and rushing soundlessly
> away out there under the arches of the bridge, round some clump
> of trees or an island, out where seabirds sit on stakes, over the
> roughened water *to become waves in the sea—I could not recover*
> *myself from that dissipation.* (279; emphasis added)

The dissipation of the self takes place despite his efforts to prevent it, in a "flooding forth without our willing it." Because of this
sudden "flooding," emotions that had characterized Bernard "a
minute ago" now fall into the water, rush down the river, and are
swept out to sea.[22] Bernard states twice, "I could not recover

myself from that dissipation." This is the crux of the passage: how should one read this failure to "recover" the self? At Hampton Court, Bernard asserts his belief that he can restore his self merely by banging a spoon against a table (225–26). But as he recalls his brush with death at Hampton Court, Bernard feels that he has lost his very self. Bernard's initial self-mocking irony about the role of the will in opposing the threat of extinction leaves a wide margin of doubt, doubt that is displayed in his story of losing parts of himself. In Bernard's memory of Hampton Court, the will itself is overcome; it proves utterly powerless. Not only does this dissipation occur despite human effort at self-unity, but this process of dissipation is described as "endless"; it repeats itself again and again. In other words, this dissipation is not a single, identifiable threat (as death, the most extreme form of self-loss, is usually imagined to be); rather, it is an ongoing, subversive process that always threatens to counter all efforts at self-unification. The phrases "I could not collect myself; I could not distinguish myself" suggest that the presumably unified self is always already marked by dissipation and fragmentation: in order to "collect myself," there must be pieces of the self to assemble; in order to "distinguish myself," there must be parts of the self that are discarded as not truly belonging. In *The Waves*, Woolf anticipates the postmodern moment when, as Butler notes, "[t]he subject as a self-identical entity is no more" (*Bodies That Matter* 230). Rhoda represents this state of always already dissipated and fragmented subjectivity; Bernard, on the other hand, is going through the process of divesting himself of his relatively established identity. Rhoda's state is clearly privileged in the novel: it is the state to which Bernard is moving throughout his narrative. When Bernard completes this process, his position and Rhoda's come together, just as the masculine and feminine languages come together.

Bernard closes this section by praising identity in its relation to sequence. But Bernard's images reinforce the idea of the constructed and unstable nature of identity despite his intention to praise it as solid and reassuring. He calls attention to a sound "like the knocking of railway trucks in a siding. That is the happy concatenation of one event following another in our lives" (234). The return to identity is reinforced by this aural signifier of sequence—one sound following another signifies "one event following another." But sequence is just as much a construct, a form that we impose upon life, as identity is a part we play. Bernard goes on in his praise of sequence: "Knock, knock, knock. Must, must, must. Must go, must sleep, must wake, must get up—sober, merciful word . . . without which we should be undone" (234). Without the imposition of human duty and human will, suggested by the imperative "must," life would have no sequence, no order. In this chant of "must, must, must" at the end of the Hampton Court meeting, Bernard states his conviction that human will is instrumental in overcoming the forces that oppose human being, and yet Bernard has just experienced a profound disintegration of his being. The threat of disorder clearly looms large for Bernard: if we were to ignore the self-imposed imperative "must, must, must," he says, we would bring about our very "undoing."[23]

As if to reinforce the questionable restoration of both identity and sequence, Woolf closes this section with an image of Bernard's self disintegrating and then reintegrating. Affected by the sounds and sights around him—"the chorus, and the spinning water and the just perceptible murmur of the breeze"—Bernard notes "we are slipping away. Little bits of ourselves are crumbling" (234–35). He believes he can simply put an end to this threat of literal bodily self-fragmentation by chanting his mantra, "we must go; must catch our train; must walk back to the station—must, must, must" (235). Bernard's firm belief in the power of "must"—the magic word that forges order and linearity out of our disordered and nonlinear lives—is both created and undermined by his own image of being bisected by a train: "Here is the station, and if the train were to cut me in two, I should come together on the further side, being one, being indivisible" (235). Bernard is so certain that his being is unified, that he is "one" and "indivisible," that he feels nothing could divide him, not even an actual severing of his body. Yet the agent of this severing—the train—is the very object that first suggested the idea of order, of one event following another. It was the sound of cars in the railway siding going "knock, knock, knock" that Bernard translated into the sound of the human imperative "must, must, must" (234). Yet, the railway cars are man-made and so their ordering is man-made as well. They only provide an image of sequence because of the imposition of the human will that manufactured them and then strung them together. By the same token, we must, as it were, order our lives by means of the imperative "must." Though sequence and order are created by human acts, they are just as easily dissolved by them. In the same way, Bernard is both fragmented and unified by his imaginary train. Bernard's lingering belief in the solidity and stability of identity is gradually undercut as he comes to further experience and understand the feminine "little language."

"I Need a Howl; a Cry": Bernard's Search for the "Little Language"

Bernard's intention in his "summing up" is to present *the* story of the lives of his friends, but his attempt to tell even one story of his own life is fractured by doubt and uncertainty from the beginning. He confesses his exhaustion and his lack of enthusiasm for storytelling in the beginning of his "summing up": "I begin to long for some little language such as lovers use, broken words, inarticulate words, like the shuffling of feet on the pavement" (238). Bernard has expressed the inadequacy of stories before, but for the first time, he explicitly desires the "little language," which he contrasts here with the orderly nature of written stories. He begins his "summing up" on a note of longing for something other than a neat summing up. This first gesture of Bernard's suggests that the "summing up" is not a lucid recapping of their lives, as several critics have argued, but, rather, is Bernard's story about his failure to submit all of his experiences and thoughts to one orderly, overarching story.

In this section, Bernard not only calls for the "little language" when his subject is one that does not lend itself to the form of a story, but he also uses fragmented and figurative language at times. In one instance when he calls for the "little language," Bernard does so because he finds that "consecutive sentences" are inadequate to describe his first love (251). Before he makes his pronouncements, his speech already resembles the fragmentary language of the emotions and the body that Jinny speaks: he piles one coordinate phrase on top of another and describes his thoughts through metaphors of bodily sensations: "Then a thunder-clap of complete indifference; the light blown out; then the return of measureless irresponsible joy . . . and then the mystic sense of completion and then that rasping, dog-fish skin-like roughness—those black arrows of shivering sensation" (250–51). Even though Bernard's language here comes close to the "little language" of sensation, his language is still quite self-conscious and discursive, and he desires something more elemental: "[B]ut what is the use of painfully elaborating these consecutive sentences when what one needs is nothing consecutive but a bark, a groan?" (251). Despite his stark realization that consecutive sentences do not and cannot convey "the flying moment of first love" (250), Bernard recuperates from this moment of frustration and failure by trying to resume his story, one made up of sentences, not of barks and groans: "But to return. *Let us again pretend* that life is a solid substance, shaped like a globe which we turn about in our fingers. *Let us pretend* that we can make out a plain and logical story, so that when one matter is despatched—love for instance—we go on, in an orderly manner, to the next" (251; emphasis added). This is a self-consciously recuperative moment: although Bernard denies the possibility of stories, wanting instead one-word expressions of feeling and sensation, he is conscious of the pretense, stating twice, "Let us pretend." Bernard has reached the point where he sees that sequential narrative is an illusion, but he also sees that it is a necessary illusion. The novel does not dispense with narrative (how could it?); rather, it opens out narrative to include its other—the fragment.

Bernard continues his reflection on the illusion of sequence in a passage in which his narrative discourse again mirrors the "voice of action." Because Bernard is telling a story *about* both stories and the "little language," his language necessarily reflects both subjects. What leads up to the passage in question is a brief reflection on the period in life when identity solidifies ("A shell forms upon the soft soul, nacreous, shiny, upon which sensations tap their beaks in vain" [255]). In other words, identity makes us impervious to sensations: Rhoda, Jinny, and Neville are the most open to sensation because they have the softest "shells," to use Bernard's metaphor.[24] Bernard's "shell" of identity, on the other hand, hardened early. For this reason, his life was orderly and regulated, but he now finds fault with the reliance upon sequence in the life marked by clear-cut identity.

But it is a mistake, this extreme precision, this orderly and military progress; a convenience, a lie. *There is always deep below it, even when we arrive punctually at the appointed time with our white waistcoats and polite formalities, a rushing stream of broken dreams, nursery rhymes, street cries, half-finished sentences and sights—elm trees, willow trees, gardeners sweeping, women writing— that rise and sink* even as we hand a lady down to dinner. While one straightens the fork so precisely on the table-cloth, a thousand faces mop and mow. There is nothing one can fish up in a spoon; nothing one can call an event. Yet it is alive too and deep, this stream. Immersed in it I would stop between one mouthful and the next, and look intently at a vase, perhaps with one red flower, while a reason struck me, a sudden revelation. (255–56; emphasis added)

Bernard is not content to "pretend that life is a solid substance" or that he "can make out a plain and logical story" (251), because even at moments when we are most aware of individual identity (signified by society in the passage above), our life is suspended precariously over a stream of disorderly and random thoughts and images that is "alive" and "deep." This stream is a loose collection of memories or visions from the past ("gardeners sweeping, women writing"), fragments from the unconscious ("broken dreams"), scraps of language and sensation ("unfinished sentences and sights"), and songs and phrases ("nursery rhymes, street cries"). This "rushing stream" is located "deep below" the "orderly and military progress" of life. But in positioning it "below" life, Woolf does not locate it outside of life: as Bernard makes clear, these images and words "rise and sink" and "mop and mow" in the midst of such a mundane act as "hand[ing] a lady down to dinner." Like the unconscious, the "rushing stream" is an accessible region of the mind, which may not be so deeply buried as we think. As I have argued above, Woolf's text locates subversive potential within, not outside of, language. Here Bernard himself discovers a different reason for the impossibility of stories: stories can never be successfully ordered and coherently shaped not because of his failure as a storyteller, as he has sometimes thought, but because when stories pretend to be coherent and complete, they do so by leaving out this "rushing stream of broken dreams."[25] The storyteller can only create the "convenient" order of stories by suppressing this stream of thoughts and images. In much the same way, masculinity and those traits associated with it become central at the expense of the repudiated feminine. At the end of the passage, the line "There is nothing one can fish up in a spoon; nothing one can call an event" may be read as a self-reflexive comment on the strange content of *The Waves*. There are no events in the novel: the characters refer to things that happen to them in the present, but these things do not seem to be taking place; they do not have the reality and immediacy of events.[26] As Bernard says, it is hard to point out something solid and substantial in the novel, or something "one can fish up in a spoon." Instead, we are given fleeting images, half-formed thoughts, and visions (like the woman writing at Elvedon or Bernard's "fin in the waste of waters") in place of the actions and events that form the substance of the Edwardian novel against which Woolf defined her own fiction.[27]

As a result of his new awareness of "the rushing stream of broken dreams," Bernard begins to experience a loss of identity, which is brought on by solitude and silence ("Let me be alone. Let me cast and throw away this veil of being" [294]). As his identity dissipates, he goes further than a desire for the "little language" or "words of one syllable." He goes so far as to want no words at all but, rather, pure vocalization, like the "bark" and "groan" he longs for in another passage:

> I need a howl; a cry. When the storm crosses the marsh and sweeps over me where I lie in the ditch unregarded I need no words. Nothing neat. Nothing that comes down with all its feet on the floor. None of those resonances and lovely echoes that break and chime from nerve to nerve in our breasts making wild music, false phrases. I have done with phrases. (295)

His lack of identity allows him to see the superfluousness of phrases, which are too neat and assured to be genuine. What Bernard wants now is silence, having finally come to see its beauty as Susan does. But Bernard soon goes beyond this desire for pure anonymity and silence: just as Jinny and Susan are capable of speaking both the "little language" of the body and the analytic language of discourse, Bernard too is able to combine words of one syllable and the sequence of story in the fabric of his tale. The result of this reconnection of opposed languages is the discovery (or creation) of a type of language that allows him access both to "the thing in itself" and to himself without the external trappings of identity.

Woolf explores what she calls "things in themselves" primarily through Bernard, Rhoda, and Neville.[28] These three characters set out on a deliberate search for a certain type of language that will bring them into unmediated relation to the world. Rhoda seeks "the thing in itself" without recourse to metaphor or simile (163); Bernard seeks the feminine "little language" as opposed to the masculine language of stories as a means of attaining the "thing in itself" (238); and Neville, who is the focus of this section, seeks a kind of fusion of speech and writing that brings together everyday and literary language. A passage from Woolf's diary gives a sense of the common link between the character's quests. This passage, written on 27 February 1926, reveals the difficulties of formulating this idea of "the thing in itself."

> Why is there not a discovery in life? Something one can lay hands on & say "This is it"? My depression is a harassed feeling—I'm looking; but that's not it—that's not it. What is it? And shall I die before I find it? . . . I have a great and astonishing sense of something there, which is "it"—It is not exactly beauty that I mean. It is that the thing is in itself enough: satisfactory; achieved . . . I do fairly frequently come upon this "it"; & then feel quite at rest . . . Is that what I meant to say? Not in the least. (*Diary* 3: 62–63)

Woolf describes in this passage her fleeting awareness that "it"— "the thing in itself"—is enough. The passage not only describes this understanding; it performs the writer's difficulty in defining this "it" in language. But what is "the thing in itself"? For Woolf in *The Waves*, "the thing in itself" refers to that which appears to the senses. Rhoda, Neville, and Bernard use the phrase "the thing in itself" to refer to concrete objects in the world, to which they gain access through sense perception. The characters typically find that language impedes their access to direct sensory experience, just as Woolf found it difficult to pin down her meaning in the diary passage. And yet, they base their search in language, for, as modern subjects, it is through language that they apprehend the world.

Woolf's difficulty in pinning down her subject is not the result of
unclear thinking; rather, the nature of her subject necessarily eludes
simple expression in language. If "the thing is in itself enough,"
isn't the attempt to describe it in language necessarily excessive?
Woolf's characters come upon the same conflict in their attempts
to get at objects in the world through language.

Rhoda longs for a concrete language of immediacy after
Percival's death, which has allowed her to see through the indi-
rection and falsity of language as she knows it. His death makes
her see life differently: the private images that Rhoda uses to escape from the terrors of daily life, such as her lack of identity, are
"clothed in ruin" now that Percival is dead (159). After welcom-
ing the overt violence around her that Percival's death has allowed
her to see, Rhoda expresses her desire for a direct language while
listening to a singer at a concert. Like the music, the language
Rhoda desires would be overt, direct, and nonrepresentational.
Rhoda uses the metaphor of the voice as an arrow aimed at an
apple tree. It seems at first that the cry or single note sung by the
woman is the type of communication that Rhoda seeks because it
hits its mark. For Rhoda, however, the cry, which Bernard seeks in
his attempt to find the "little language" in his "summing up," is
inadequate: "She has provided us with a cry. But only with a cry.
And what is a cry?" (162–63). But Rhoda soon realizes that language sometimes provides direct access to concrete objects, precisely the thing she has been seeking.

Rhoda wants to perceive the thing—in this case, music—as it
exists in the world immediately, without language mediating between herself and the thing. It is the need to use simile in order to
convey the qualities of things that she critiques, and yet she uses
simile and metaphor to describe the music:

> "Like" and "like" and "like"—but what is the thing that lies be-
> neath the semblance of the thing? Now that lightning has gashed
> the tree and the flowering branch has fallen and Percival, by his
> death, has made me this gift, let me see the thing. There is a
> square; there is an oblong. The players take the square and place
> it upon the oblong. They place it very accurately. They make a
> perfect dwelling-place. (163)

Percival's death has allowed her to get beneath appearances to "the thing," which is a structure of some sort—a square placed upon an oblong that forms "a dwelling-place." Although Rhoda wants to be able to describe the thing in itself without the use of figurative language, she inadvertently uses metaphor. The musicians are creating sound, not a "dwelling-place" made of squares and oblongs. Nevertheless, Rhoda is satisfied that she has captured the thing in itself. The dwelling-place will be mentioned later by Susan as a metaphor for life: "I have seen life in blocks, substantial, huge; its battlements and towers . . . a dwelling-place made from time immemorial after an hereditary pattern" (215). Susan takes for granted this reassuring image of life as dwelling-place or shelter; it is not something that she has struggled to achieve. Rhoda, however, can only perceive life in this way through effort after the shock of Percival's death. It is death that allows Rhoda to arrive at this basic level of language where "the thing is in itself enough."

Twice in his summing up, Bernard turns to the idea of the "thing in itself," and both instances are connected with death or the loss of identity. As it does for Rhoda, Percival's death gives Bernard a sense of things in themselves, separated from their connotations and connections. Bernard describes his vision of the world on the first morning after Percival's death in this way: "To see things without attachment, from the outside, and to realise their beauty in itself—how strange!" (263). Before his experience of death, Bernard could only realize the beauty of things by means of his beautiful phrases for them: until this moment, "things without attachment" held little interest for him.

When Bernard experiences "things in themselves" the second time, it is not in the context of death but of solitude, silence, and the loss of identity. The "little language" and "things in themselves" are both starkly opposed to phrases at this point, since Bernard has just declared himself "done with phrases" (295). Silence, solitude, and anonymity allow him to see beyond the accretions of language that surround objects in the world. Finally, he arrives at a vision of the thing in itself: "How much better is silence; the coffee-cup, the table. How much better to sit by myself like the solitary sea-bird that opens its wings on the stake. Let me sit here for ever with bare things, this coffee-cup, this knife, this fork, things in themselves, *myself being myself*" (295; emphasis added). Here Bernard attains a state of being that resembles that of Jinny and Susan: he is immersed in sense perceptions; he uses a simple, basic language. Yet he need not trade in his subjectivity, his participation in the symbolic order, in order to attain this state. (In the same way, Jinny and Susan are fully capable of symbolic discourse, though they claim they are not, as we saw above.) What is interesting is that though Bernard remains firmly *in* the symbolic, he is able to experience a loss of identity so great that he sees the world in a different way: just as the "rushing stream of broken dreams" breaks through and disrupts the "orderly progress" of life and of stories, so this identityless state that opens onto the world of "bare things" becomes possible to a *man with a self*. For Bernard *is himself* here, as he emphasizes at the end of the passage, where, through apposite phrases, he likens "myself being myself" to "things in themselves." This final acceptance of identity is only possible because while sitting with "bare things . . . things in themselves," he remains silent rather than producing phrases to describe the things that surround him. When we do not name something, he implies, it exists, it is itself. When we name it, it is changed, just as Neville realizes when he attempts to write a poem.

Although Bernard has spent his whole life in the act of changing things by naming them and making phrases about them in an attempt to know love, the moon, or death, he now realizes that things are only known in themselves when we don't make them part of a story, but allow them to exist as they are. Bernard uses "words of one syllable"—"this knife, this fork"—such as Susan or Jinny might use. Here the "little language" is not the language of emotions but language at its most basic level—single words that describe simple everyday objects. In this instance, the "little language" is associated not with the complete loss of identity, but with identity at its most basic level. Bernard is "himself being himself," not "Bernard" the phrase-maker, the man who was once Byron, who has a wife, etc. The trappings of identity such as profession, family, and social connection are pared away and left behind. Bernard now is merely himself in the sense that he is the meeting place of certain faculties.

Woolf wants to arrive at what is irreducible in subjectivity, that without which there is no self, and this proves to be sense perceptions and the language in which they are stated. The novel first suggests a connection between this pared-down identity and the "little language" at the beginning of the summing up when Bernard "long[s] for some little language such as lovers use, broken words, inarticulate words" (238). At this moment, he rejects the certainty and "neat design" of stories, wanting instead "some design more in accordance with those moments of humiliation and triumph that come now and then undeniably" (239). One such moment involves Bernard lying in a ditch watching the clouds, which for him represent the side of nature that is opposed to the human: as he watches the clouds, he is delighted by "the confusion, the height, the indifference, and the fury" (239). Bernard describes his position vis-à-vis the clouds in this way: "towering, trailing, broken off, lost, and I forgotten, minute, in a ditch. Of story, of design I do not see a trace then" (239). The "I" is "forgotten," but it is not dissipated, as Bernard describes his feeling of self-loss at Hampton Court (279). That sensation of the self fragmenting and falling away is not a state that the novel describes as desirable: Rhoda's anguish attests to this. Self-dissipation is inevitable, however; as Bernard notes, it is "endless." What Woolf is tracing in the "summing up" is the possibility of a state in which identity is subsumed but not erased: "I" is "forgotten," but it may be retrieved. This state in which the external trappings of identity are suppressed allows Bernard access to a different type of language and to a different relation to the world. No longer imposing his "arbitrary design" on the world, Bernard is now able to see "things in themselves," which he, Neville, and Rhoda have all desired, and he is only able to arrive at this state through struggling to attain the "little language" of women and combining it with the story of his life.

"This difference . . . this identity . . . was overcome": The Meeting of Masculine and Feminine

In the course of his summing up, Bernard undergoes such a profound loss of identity that he describes himself as "a man without a self" (285). What makes this experience of self-loss different from the many similar moments that Bernard has already experienced is that he now embraces and celebrates self-loss. Before, Bernard was caught unawares by his various moments of self-fragmentation; at Hampton Court, for instance, he also attempted to "recover" from "that dissipation" (279). But in his summing up, Bernard calls for the loss of self; he actively wants to stop being Bernard in conjunction with his call for "a little language." Bernard opens the summing up with a reflection on those moments when "I" is "forgotten," when he has no identity. He longs for a "little language" in order to be able to speak of such moments authentically. When Bernard experiences the death of the self, the moment of full self-loss for which these other experiences have paved the way, it is accompanied by the loss of his ability to speak and write.[29] His "death of the self" has as much to do with the depletion of linguistic abilities as with the loss of his identity.

The central role played by language in the creation of selfhood becomes clear when Bernard notes that the self that provides opposition, the one that bangs the spoon on the table, is silent when he calls upon it: "This self now as I leant over the gate looking down over fields rolling in waves of colour beneath me made no answer. He threw up no opposition. He attempted no phrase. His fist did not form . . . No fin breaks the waste of this immeasurable sea. Life has destroyed me. No echo comes when I speak, no varied words" (284–85). The "fin" that fails to appear is a thought; the "immeasurable sea" is the blankness of Bernard's mind, or the blankness of the world when it is not marked by the variations of thought. Language is constitutive of identity: without speech, without "varied words," Bernard is no one. It is this wordless state that Bernard describes as being "a man without a self . . . A dead man" (285). Bernard then looks back on his life from this altered perspective. His past and his friends' pasts, which are the subject of this summing up, have lost their weight and substance as a result of his self-loss. He now sees himself, the world, and their lives as empty:

> The woods had vanished; the earth was a waste of shadow . . . A man without a self, I said. A heavy body leaning on a gate. A dead man. With dispassionate despair, with entire disillusionment I surveyed the dust dance; my life, my friends' lives, and those fabulous presences, men with brooms, women writing, the

> willow tree by the river—clouds and phantoms made of dust
> too, of dust that changed . . . mutable, vain. (285)

These once-reassuring images that he has conjured up again and
again throughout his life now reveal themselves as purely imaginary, transitory, and temporary. Bernard mourns the fact that he
has founded his life upon the slim basis of the imagination; and
yet, now that his imagination is gone, he mourns its loss as well.
His loss of language—his inability to leave a mark on what he
sees around him—leaves the world "empty" and "colourless":
"The heaviness of my despondency . . . pushed me, an elderly
man, a heavy man with grey hair, through the colourless field, the
empty field. *No more to hear echoes, no more to see phantoms, to conjure up no opposition,* but to walk always unshadowed *making no
impress upon the dead earth*" (285; emphasis added). In other words,
Bernard has no language (he is "no more to hear echoes" of his
own words), no imagination (he is "no more to see phantoms"),
no intellect (he will "conjure up no opposition"), and thus no self
(he will "walk always unshadowed"). Subjectivity then is defined
primarily by the capacity for language. For Woolf, identity at its
most basic level is defined as a sign-making activity, and the signs
that it makes are written ones: when Bernard has lost his identity,
he "mak[es] no impress upon the dead earth." In other words, the
very fact of being involves making an imprint, making tracks, signs
that, like writing, are marks or impressions upon a physical substance.[30] The figure of the self as a shadow, an image of the self
that is somehow other, also suggests the way in which selfhood is
constituted by otherness. This image recalls Bernard's and Rhoda's
reflections on the construction of a persona for the eyes of others.
      As a "man without a self," but returned to the world on some
level, Bernard finds that no language is simple or spare enough to
describe his perspective as a man without a self.

> But how describe the world seen without a self? There are no
> words. Blue, red—even they distract, even they hide with thick-
> ness instead of letting the light through. How describe or say
> anything in articulate words again?—save that it fades, save that
> it undergoes a gradual transformation, becomes, even in the
> course of one short walk, habitual—this scene also. (287)

Bernard's characteristic desire to describe and narrate things and events around him persists despite his aphasia. He wants to "describe the world seen without a self," but finds that "[t]here are no words." At this point, even the monosyllabic "little language" is too obtrusive: his words cover things "instead of letting the light through" (287).[31] Now that his self has vanished, he does not know how he can "describe or say anything in articulate words again." He considers his connection to the others:

> Am I all of them? Am I one and distinct? I do not know. We sat here together. But now Percival is dead, and Rhoda is dead; we are divided; we are not here. Yet I cannot find any obstacle separating us. There is no division between me and them. As I talked I felt, "I am you." This difference we make so much of, this identity we so feverishly cherish, was overcome. (288–89)[32]

Although this remark could be read as an indication of the union of six separate identities, as such remarks often are in the criticism, division stands out most of all. If Bernard perceives a union, it is by default, for he only fails to find obstacles and divisions: he does not state that they do not exist. Moreover, identity itself, the tendency toward individuality, is no longer an obstacle: "[T]his identity," Bernard declares, "was overcome." That is, their identities are not joined: they no longer, strictly speaking, have identities. Bernard's great sense of loss, his feeling of being beyond life, is clear from his remark "All this little affair of 'being' is over" (288). Later, Bernard again links the loss of identity with the end of being: "Heaven be praised for solitude . . . Let me cast and throw away this veil of being, this cloud that changes with the least breath . . . Now no one may see me and I change no more. Heaven be praised for solitude that has removed the pressure of the eye, the solicitation of the body, and all need of lies and phrases" (294). Bernard realizes at last the weak foundation of identity. Again, it is solitude and silence that allow him to be no one, and language that requires him to be some one, to have a unified identity. Bernard's understanding of language thus undergoes a profound transformation in the summing up, a transformation that is caused by his awareness of the need to reconnect feminine and masculine languages.

This reconnection is mirrored by other reconnections that occur in the summing up: in Bernard, fragments and stories are conjoined as well as masculine and feminine identities. These reconnections are figured in a pair of powerful metaphors involving women that Bernard uses toward the end of the novel. As Bernard nears the end of his "summing up" and welcomes the loss of his identity, he says that he is giving up storytelling completely (but, of course, he is still telling a story about giving up stories). Interestingly, this tale of the renunciation of stories depends upon two figures of women. First, Bernard leaves his book of phrases to be cleaned up by the charwoman: "My book, stuffed with phrases, has dropped to the floor. It lies under the table to be swept up by the charwoman when she comes wearily at dawn looking for scraps of paper . . . to be swept up" (294–95). Mrs. Moffat, Bernard's charwoman, has performed a similar function before, and is one of Woolf's privileged figures of working-class women who are invested with a great deal of textual power. The reference to the book of phrases being "swept up" also brings to mind Bernard's childhood image of the lady writing and the gardeners sweeping at Elvedon, his imaginary mythical land. The genders of the writer and the sweeper are now reversed: Bernard has taken the place of the woman writer who haunts the early pages of the novel, much in the same way that he has displaced the now absent Rhoda, and a charwoman now takes the place of the male gardeners.

But a metaphor of a woman writing makes its way back into the text in Bernard's further thoughts on his renunciation of writing. Bernard remarks with exhaustion:

> What is the phrase for the moon? And the phrase for love? By what name are we to call death? I do not know. I need a little language such as lovers use, words of one syllable such as children speak when they come into the room and find their mother sewing and pick up some scrap of bright wool, a feather, or a shred of chintz. I need a howl; a cry. (295)

Bernard is no longer able to produce witty phrases that capture the essence of lofty emotions and events such as "love" and "death," the very phrases that fill his now discarded book, which

Mrs. Moffat sweeps up. Instead, he needs the monosyllabic words of lovers and children. Bernard describes the children's actions, which mirror the "words of one syllable" that they speak. Entering a room and finding their mother sewing, the children finger the scraps that she leaves behind. Like the fragments of fabric the mother casts aside, the children's words are fragments. They speak disconnected "words of one syllable," the "little language such as lovers use," which has been identified as feminine throughout the novel. The fact that the mother is sewing is critical to the passage, since sewing, like weaving and tying, is a figure for narration.[33] The children's one-syllable words resemble the scraps that the mother has cut out of her fabric, or the parts that she has removed from her story, and, by analogy, the feminine that has been "cut out of," or repressed, in Western culture. But when the children pick up these scraps, they are, in effect, speaking in fragments to their mother, who listens to them and works those words back into the "fabric" of the story she is telling/sewing. That is, the feminine fragment is restored or recovered. Woolf's mother figure is an artist figure on several levels: although Woolf does not specify what she is making, we can assume that, like many products of women's domestic arts, it has a caretaking function: it may be a quilt, a coat, or a hat. Her work of art is both decorative and functional and perhaps communicative as well: the mother may leave a signature or other sign on a border, or use a favorite color of the wearer. The centrality of this figure to the text as a whole is evident in several ways: Woolf uses the key term the "little language" to identify the verbal exchange between the mother and her children. And, most importantly, this imagined scene is an inspiration to Bernard. He not only wants but *needs* to be like the children who speak to their mother at work. Just as the children and their mother connect fragment and story, feminine and masculine, so Bernard does over the course of his summing up by linking phrases and fragments and by conveying his need for fragments in phrases.[34] Moreover, only by letting go of his preoccupation with linear narrative is Bernard able to give up his fixation with unitary identity. As this kind of storyteller, one who is able to merge "words of one syllable" with the fabric of the larger story, like the mother who reintegrates her children's fragments into her story,

Bernard becomes a differently gendered being, one in whom mas-culine and feminine coexist.

The way in which we attribute Bernard's gender must be in dispute at this point—we need to ask if he is a he or a she, and what the ramifications are of this gender fluidity. Furthermore, what allows for Bernard's assumption of a feminine subject posi-tion—one that is defined by the loss, rather than the possession, of identity—and with it, a feminine language? And how do we describe a man who assumes a feminine subject position? Is this being then a woman? Thoughts of Rhoda, particularly of her death, seem to enable a number of Bernard's transformations. It is essen-tial to note that only after reporting on Rhoda's suicide is Bernard fully able to experience the world as "a man without a self" (285) and to speak the feminine "little language."[35] It seems that Bernard loses his self and gains the feminine language by appropriating the now empty spot that Rhoda once occupied. Bernard himself comments on the particular connection between himself and Rhoda when he notes that he once "evoked to serve as opposite to myself the figure of Rhoda always so furtive, always with fear in her eyes, always seeking some pillar in the desert, to find which she had gone; she had killed herself" (281). Thinking of their dif-ferences paradoxically leads him to note their connection, and they are both divided and connected through her suicide. As he imag-ines urging Rhoda not to commit suicide, he realizes that he is also convincing himself: "In persuading her I was also persuad-ing my own soul. For this is not one life; nor do I always know if I am man or woman, Bernard or Neville, Louis, Susan, Jinny or Rhoda—so strange is the contact of one with another" (281). If we as readers leave Bernard's gender in question, we are only follow-ing Bernard's lead, for, as he states, he himself does not always know if he is man or woman.

Rhoda's experiences of self-loss or the dissipation of identity throughout the novel are echoed by Bernard's similar experiences in his summing up. Just as Rhoda cannot conceive of the merging of moment and moment (222), Bernard now fails to make the moments of their lives merge into a story; just as Rhoda lacks a face (122), Bernard's features now become blurred as he loses his identity. Yet, while Bernard's self-fragmentation is quite extensive,

Rhoda's reaches much further because of the impact it has on her. Rhoda is tormented by her inability to create an identity in the first place; Bernard, on the other hand, rejoices in his ability to gradually shed his well-established identity. Rhoda's failure to create an identity finally leads her to commit suicide; Bernard's success in shedding his, on the other hand, allows him to face the possibility of death with triumph.

Bernard's metamorphosis into a displaced modern subject in need of "a howl; a cry" (295) is possible not only because of what he has learned from Susan's and Jinny's "little language," but also because of what he has learned from Rhoda. For this reason, we could read Bernard's loss of identity and access to the feminine "little language" in his summing up as possible only through a masculine displacement of the feminine. That is, Bernard gains access to the "little language" and his position of dissolved subjectivity through the displacement of Rhoda. But Rhoda has already fully anticipated Bernard's narrative move: her subjectivity includes both feminine and masculine sides, because she has not only lived that marginal position but has also narrated it, just as Bernard eventually does. Far from silent, Rhoda speaks a highly analytical language in which she examines her own lack of identity and her search for a language that will give her access to "things in themselves." Like Jinny and Susan, Rhoda occupies a feminine subject position, and, like them, she does so not in a simple, clear-cut way, for she is able to reflect on this position, on her lack of identity. Rhoda may, in a sense, suffer a textual violence in being written out of the novel as a suicide, but this is tempered by that fact that this displacement is followed by the incorporation of the feminine language in the text's concluding narrative (Bernard's "summing up") and the incorporation of a feminine subject position by the novel's central male character.[36]

With its delineation of both a masculine and feminine language and a masculine and feminine subject position, *The Waves* could be read as subscribing to a system of gender based on a binary opposition between masculine and feminine. Although such a reading is suggestive, Bernard, who seems to be fully in command of his identity, experiences a dissipation of identity so severe that he becomes "a man without a self." We may read Bernard's accession to the position of a "man without a self" as constituting a kind of masculine displacement of the feminine, but such a reading depends upon a binary notion of gender. In order to become a "man without a self," Bernard must become a man who is a woman, a feminized man. And the feminization of man operates by means of the appropriation of woman's place or nonplace as a subject.[37] However, this reading is difficult to maintain given that Bernard's doubts about identity and stories precede Rhoda's death. That is, Bernard represents the masculine subject as author(ity) at the same time that this position is marked by fragmentation. Bernard is, in some way, always already not Bernard, that is, not in command of his words and his self. Subjectivity itself, including masculine subjectivity, is continually threatened by fragmentation and disintegration in the novel. Similarly, the text both relies upon the gender binary in its positing of gender-marked languages and questions the gender binary in its connection of these languages. As readers, we are led to read gender at the same time that this process of reading gender is thwarted by the text through the suspension of Bernard's gender. It is through this doubled process that Woolf creates her visionary view of gender: the text's refusal of simple opposition requires the reader to refuse simple opposition as well. Let's reconsider Bernard's claim "I [do not] always know if I am man or woman" (281). Given this, we cannot continue to simply identify Bernard as a man; and yet we cannot simply identify him as a woman. Given Bernard's sense of his blurred identity, we cannot simply say that Rhoda is eliminated from the text. She remains, both in and as Bernard.

This simultaneous invocation and refusal of opposition is captured by Woolf's powerful metaphor of the mother who sews and tells stories and thereby connects masculine and feminine languages. This figure may also be read as a metaphor for Bernard's transformation into a being of fluid and indeterminate gender, who may be *either* man or woman or *both* man and woman. Although Bernard has reached this point only through his displacement of Rhoda, he incorporates and therefore preserves Rhoda's feminine subjectivity in his new self, just as he incorporates Susan's and Jinny's "little language" with the masculine language of sequential narrative. This reintegration of story and fragment, masculine and feminine, puts into question the construction of gender as a fixed and stable opposition as well as the gendering of different levels of discourse. Woolf has turned the violence of masculine displacement to feminine—or, rather, feminist—ends, by reinscribing the stark opposition between genders as a fluid reintegration of genders.

Woolf's reintegration of masculine with feminine, her refusal of opposition, has broad ramifications in this age of divisive identity politics. At a time when difference is typically either insisted upon or ignored, it is important to realize that difference must also be questioned, and this is precisely what Woolf does. The result of the various connections delineated in *The Waves*—of identities, languages, and concepts—is that identity boundaries are blurred, and difference is put into question. Such questioning or suspension of difference leads to a more fruitful exchange between the genders, which is impossible when they are starkly opposed. Masculine and feminine are able to come into play and play off each other as well as to inflect each other. In *The Waves*, Woolf sketches the contours of a new state of being in which difference no longer represents an obstacle or battlefield but instead a fertile ground of exchange.

THREE

"THE THIRD SEX"
Figures of Inversion
in Djuna Barnes's Nightwood

"Am I not the girl to know of what I speak?"
—Djuna Barnes, *Nightwood*

Dr. Matthew O'Connor, the voluble storyteller of Djuna Barnes's novel *Nightwood*, spins tales on the subjects of woman's sexuality, homosexuality, desire, and love, spouting wild anecdotes, bitter laments, and intricate theories in a series of densely metaphorical monologues addressed primarily to a woman. By means of the figure of the doctor, a transvestite gynecologist, and his theories, the novel conceives of gender identity as an open-ended range of possibilities rather than as a strict choice between masculine or feminine. Matthew bases his theories of gender and sexuality on two ambiguously gendered characters—Robin Vote, the girl who looks like a boy, and himself.

Matthew's gender ambiguity has a strong impact on his position as a storyteller and on his narrative authority. In a sense, Matthew is an authoritative male speaker who aims to explain the intricacies of inversion to Nora Flood, Robin's lover. That is, Matthew speaks with the authority of his masculine subjectivity and his status as a doctor. But these traditional bases of authority are blatantly undercut by the fact that he is a would-be woman and an unlicensed quack.[1] By portraying Matthew as a transvestite gynecologist/theorist, Barnes creates a biting parody of the figure of the sexologist whose aim is to define the nature of female inversion. The theorist's interest, however, is found to be more than theoretical: Matthew studies women in order to satisfy his desire to be a woman. Matthew's own ambiguous gender position

63

allows him to question the gender binary and to construct more complex models of fluid gender identifications on the wide-ranging gender spectrum.

Matthew devises several theoretical models for inversion that throw both masculine and feminine radically into question.[2] The gender of the invert or "the third sex" consists of a vacillation between masculine and feminine, regardless of biological sex. By making the relation between sex and gender asymmetrical and indeterminate, the text denaturalizes the supposed congruence between sex and gender that is promoted by means of the gender binary. The invert thus provides a way of breaking open the closed and symmetrical binary opposition between masculine and feminine and challenging the idea of the binary opposition on which gender has been understood to rest. In a textual doubling of sexual inversion, the invert is inscribed in the text by means of the rhetorical figure of the chiasmus, a figure that consists of a double inversion.[3] Matthew attempts to determine the truth of inversion in these formulae, but the shifting, unstable nature of his own formulae undoes his quest for the truth. What happens to gender in this process? Matthew's figures of inversion rely to some extent on the gender binary at the same time that they question and undo it, an ambiguity that I will explore below. Matthew thus becomes a kind of deconstructive theorist of inversion, but at the same time he is a parody of the sexologist whose discourse relies upon and confirms the gender binary. This ambiguity can be seen especially in Matthew's transvestism. While on the one hand Matthew is sophisticated in his reading of gender ambiguity, particularly its manifestations in inversion, on the other hand he uses the feminine masquerade as a means of arriving at an end—being a woman. Other strands of the text also work to question this reliance upon the masculine/feminine opposition. First, Robin Vote, as a representation of the feminine, escapes any attempt to pin her down.[4] Finally and most importantly, Matthew's own figures for inversion undermine not just the truth of inversion, in that the gender of the invert is left undecidable and indeterminate, but they also render undecidable the truth of gender, or the simple binary scheme upon which gender is based. The constructed nature of gender in the invert is not just a special case of gender ambiguity;

instead, it points to the constructed and ambiguous nature of all gender identity.

As the title of the novel implies, the night is the space in which the novel takes place. "Night" is also the valorized term of a series of terms synonymous with the feminine that are found in the oppositions night and day, irrational and rational, unconscious and conscious, improper and proper, and anonymity and identity. Barnes takes these classical binary oppositions governing Western thought and inverts the hierarchies, privileging the feminine term: the night, the irrational, the unconscious, the improper, the anonymous.[5] The novel's key scenes unfold in the night; Nora is engaged in a search for the meaning of the night so that she may understand Robin; Matthew is a theorist of the night, who explains its meaning to Nora. Robin, who is practically synonymous with the night, is actually at the bottom of Nora's search. Since Robin's character, and that of the invert for which she is the figure, is so intertwined with the night, both Nora and the reader must first come to an understanding of the night in order to understand Robin. Since the night erases identity, as we come to know the night and Robin we will come, paradoxically, to understand Robin less, or to question our knowledge at every turn.

"The Night, 'Beware of That Dark Door!'"

In the following passage, Nora describes the shift from understanding the night in its ordinary sense to understanding the night in its fullest sense: "'I used to think,' Nora said, 'that people just went to sleep, or if they did not go to sleep that they were themselves, but now—... now I see that the night does something to a person's identity, even when asleep'" (81).[6] Nora seems overwhelmed here by the night's transformative power, having witnessed its effects primarily on Robin, and on other night people whom she has encountered while searching for Robin on the streets of Paris. As we will see over the course of this chapter, Nora has the sensibility of the day: she believes in the clarity and lucidity of life. Consequently, Nora once thought that the night had little or no effect on a person, that one slept or remained "oneself" during the night.

But she gradually has come to see that the night's effects are so great that they can lead to the erasure of identity, as is the case with Robin.

In *Nightwood* identity, meaning the sameness and oneness of the self, is repeatedly undone and erased by the force of the night and the anonymity that is associated with it. Barnes's text is the opposite of the discourse of sameness: with otherness and multiplicity as its key terms, it works at undoing sameness.[7] In *Nightwood*, coherent identity is a fiction that only comes to be through a repression of otherness. Nora, associated with the day, reason, clear-cut identity, and gender certainty, is drawn to Robin, associated with the night, sexuality, anonymity, and gender ambiguity. Through her connection to Robin and the night, Nora herself begins to change, to question her belief in the day and all that it implies.

Robin's lack of identity, her difference not only from others but also from herself, has a great effect on her lovers. Love is generally thought of as familiarity with another, or as immersion in another's identity, but in *Nightwood*, the lack of identity seems to inspire love. Nora, Felix, and Jenny are drawn to Robin's lack of identity, but each creates an identity for her, expecting her to take it on as her own. Robin, then, is an empty sign that can stand for anything. Felix makes Robin "the Baronin," and they have a child, as he wishes. But Robin rejects the child along with the title and Felix's obsession with the past, which he imagines that Robin shares or embodies. Anonymity plays a role in Robin's relationship with Jenny as well. Since Jenny herself lacks an identity, she wishes to absorb identity from Robin and to use Robin and Nora's love in a secondhand way; hence, her nickname is the "squatter" (65–67). In "The Possessed," when Robin begins to wander in the direction of Nora's house, and away from Jenny, she begins to shed her identity even more: "Because Robin's engagements were with something unseen, because in her speech and her gestures there was a desperate anonymity, Jenny became hysterical" (168). Nora is drawn to Robin's lack of will and motive when they meet at the circus. After introducing herself, Robin "looked about her distractedly. 'I don't want to be here.' But it was all she said; she did not explain where she wished to be" (55). The next time they are mentioned, they are lovers, and one can gather that it was Nora who initiated the relationship, since Robin characteristically lets herself be carried along by the will of another. The only actions that are characteristic of Robin are leaving, wandering, and straying. In Robin's relationship with Nora, anonymity is posited as the opposite of love: "[Robin] stayed with Nora until the midwinter. Two spirits were working in her, love and anonymity. Yet they were so 'haunted' of each other that separation was impossible" (55). Robin's anonymity—her lack of a name, which stands for her lack of identity—is a force or a "spirit" that pulls her away from Nora, just as love draws her to Nora. Although Robin's lovers have sought her out because of her lack of identity, which allows them to project their desires upon her, when she fails to adopt their projected personae and remains anonymous they cannot tolerate it. This is because Robin's anonymity, a product of the night, threatens the reason and clarity of the day where the proper holds sway. The disparity between Robin and her lovers is also seen in their very different desires: Robin's three lovers want to love her (love, too, is associated with the day), but Robin cannot return love or even accept it. For Robin, there is only sex and desire. Just as love belongs to the day, sex belongs to the night and the two are distinct opposites in the world of *Nightwood*.

Since the night is the force that has created Robin and is the force that controls her, Nora becomes preoccupied with understanding the mystery of the night. She turns to Matthew to tell of her love and to learn about the night. Nora consults Matthew because he is a frequenter of the cafés and the streets and, thus, is a night person in the literal sense. In the course of their dialogues, Nora discovers that Matthew's understanding of the night does not arise from mere observation, but from a closer connection with the night, for the night's transformative power is strong. While expounding upon exemplary "French nights," Matthew remarks, "Ask Dr. Mighty O'Connor; the reason the doctor knows everything is because he's been everywhere at the wrong time and has now become anonymous" (82). Matthew, then, has a privileged understanding of Robin and the night because he too is anonymous, a condition that results from contact with the night. In Matthew's case, anonymity takes a different form than it does with Robin. That he has "been everywhere at the wrong time" suggests that his anonymity is the result of a multiplicity of identities arising from contact with many identities and locales, rather than of an erasure of identity, as is the case with Robin. Matthew possesses a number of personae in the novel: the doctor, the drinker, the tale-teller, the petty thief, the socialite, and the transvestite. Although Robin, strictly speaking, lacks an identity, this very lack also results in a multiplicity of identities (the personae her lovers impose upon her), making her very similar to Matthew.

Just as Nora discovers that Matthew has a much closer connection to the night than she had imagined, she also discovers that the night has a much richer meaning than she had formerly realized. As mentioned above, she now sees that the night "does something to a person's identity." The night seems an enigma, a mystery that she must learn more about. In this respect, the reader's relation to the night is similar to Nora's relation to it in the novel: the night, this rich sign, is a mystery to the reader as well. Robin Vote, who is closely tied to the night, lies behind all of Nora's questions in this section, and in the next dialogue between Nora and Matthew, Robin is the explicit focus. Robin, too, is an enigma that the reader is determined to solve, as is Nora.

Matthew becomes the audience for Nora's lament, and Nora becomes the audience for Matthew's monologues about the night. Although they seem to be engaged in a dialogue, Nora and Matthew are for the most part delivering two separate, intertwined monologues. Although Matthew always circles back to the topic of Robin, his words wander far and Nora often tries to pull him back to her problems. Matthew explains his meandering narrative in "Watchman, What of the Night?" in this way: "My mind is so rich that it is always wandering" (105).[8] His monologues contain biblical references, diatribes on the nature of existence, catalogs of night people, tales of his experiences on the streets, and a character sketch of Jenny, and all of this leads in some way to "the narrative of the one particular night that makes all other nights seem like something quite decent enough" (99). This is the night that Robin meets Jenny and their relationship begins. But this narrative is almost lost in the shuffle: as Matthew says, "I have a narrative, but you will be put to it to find it" (97).

Matthew begins his discourse on the night by speaking of the "polarity of times and times" (80), for in order to explain the night to Nora, he must begin by comparing it to its polar opposite, the day. Yet he immediately switches terms, referring to the close connection of night and day: "[T]he day and the night are related by their division. The very constitution of twilight is a fabulous reconstruction of fear, fear bottom-out and wrong-side up. Every day is thought upon and calculated, but the night is not premeditated" (80). Twilight, the hairline between day and night, is a "reconstruction of fear" in the sense that as creatures accustomed to the day, we fear the night, and this fear is "reconstructed" with each sunset. But this fear of the night is "bottom-out and wrongside up"—it is misguided because we do not even know what we fear about the night. Fear is turned inside out and upside down when it is associated with the night because fear is foreign to the night: it is only the mind overtaken by the perspective of the day that fears the night. The danger, darkness, and implicit violence of the night are things that the night person welcomes, rather than fears. Especially for Matthew, fear of the night is misguided because the night is his domain. As he insists in the opening pages of "Watchman," we should think about the night and we should think of it as one with the day. There is a negative sense to "every day is thought upon and calculated": the day is predictable in that it meets our expectations, while the night is "not premeditated" in that it follows no plan. Matthew nonetheless urges Nora—and, by extension, the reader or any interlocutor—to turn her thoughts to the night, because the night allows for a different kind of thinking that is not "calculating."

In speaking of the night, he uses the French as an example, for their nights "are those which nations seek the world over" (82). French nights have attained this fame because the French think of the night as one with the day, and, according to Matthew, this is the way to understand the night. He explains:

> "'The night and day are two travels, and the French—gut-greedy and fist-tight though they often are—alone leave testimony of the two in the dawn; we tear up the one for the sake of the other; not so the French.
>
> "'And why is that; because they think of the two as one continually and keep it before their mind as the monks who repeat, 'Lord Jesus Christ, Son of God, have mercy upon me!' " (82–83)

The dawn marks the connection between night and day, like twilight in the passage above. The French, unlike the Americans, "leave testimony" of both night and day in the dawn, in the sense that they are willing to declare their experience of the night. Americans, on the other hand, sacrifice the night for the sake of the day: they would not admit to a knowledge of the night, as the French would. The French also think and experience the day and the night together: they do not see a division between the two as Americans do.[9] The reference to monks in prayer emphasizes the way in which day and night are bound up in each other, just as the Christian God is a triune God, and Christ is at once human and divine. The French must ask for mercy, like the monks in prayer, because of their acknowledgment of their experience of the night, the locus of desire, crime, and multiple identities.

The inseparable connection between binary oppositions that structures the novel as a whole can be seen in a comment of Nora's explaining her attraction to Robin: "There's something evil in me that loves evil and degradation—purity's black backside!" (135). Nora is associated with the good: she searches for love and happiness; she tries to redeem Robin. The mere fact that she loves evil constitutes a close coupling between good and evil. Barnes's phrase—"purity's black backside"—is an excellent metaphor for both evil and for purity conceived not as the opposite of evil but as its repression. It is in "Go Down, Matthew" that Nora comes to this realization that she loves "purity's black backside." At this meeting between Nora and Matthew, their relation to each other is very different than it was in "Watchman." Here, Matthew seeks out Nora because he needs to unburden himself of his pain, whereas Nora was formerly the supplicant (133). By this point in the novel, Nora's understanding of Robin and of the night has grown a great deal: she is no longer the innocent seeking advice of the expert. What has led to this change is her confrontation with Jenny, at whose apartment she finds the doll that Robin once gave her (140). The doll, which I will examine in greater detail below, becomes an important focus of both Nora's and Matthew's thoughts in this section, for it signals the transference of Robin's love for Nora to another woman and it functions as a figure for "the third sex" for Matthew.

In this chapter, Nora introduces the subject of sleep, which is taken up by Matthew, who then develops further theories on the effect of the night (as sleep) on people. Nora learns, first of all, that she has little effect on Robin: the night is the controlling influence in Robin's life, not Nora or anyone else. Nora tells Matthew a story of striking Robin to wake her up. Through this act, Nora imagines that she corrupted Robin, because in sleep she had always "managed to keep whole" (145). By blaming herself for blighting Robin's "wholeness," Nora makes herself out to be instrumental in Robin's life, as if she has helped to form Robin. But Matthew sets her straight on this account: "Robin is not in your life, you are in her dream, you'll never get out of it" (146). As Matthew points out, it is Robin who controls Nora, for she has been brought into Robin's dream, her night, and her wanderings through the city. Nora, too, now wanders through the streets in search of Robin, or for a trace of her in other people (61). And Matthew now includes Nora in his list of the types "who turn the day into the night," including among them "that most miserable, the lover who watches all night in fear and anguish," as Nora watches for Robin (94).

Actually, it is Nora who first uses this metaphor of being trapped in another's dream: "'[Robin] was in her own nightmare. I tried to come between and save her, but *I was like a shadow in her dream* that could never reach her in time, as the cry of a sleeper has no echo, myself echo struggling to answer'" (145; emphasis added). Caught in Robin's nightmare, Nora is powerless to reach Robin in her attempt to save her. Nora's voice is reduced to an echo: she can only mimic another's speech, for one effect of the night is a loss of voice, identity, and power. Her loss of identity is figured by the simile "I was like a shadow in her dream": not only is Nora a figure in a waking dream, but she is a mere shadow, or the trace of an object created by an effect of light. Nora has failed to impose her life or her standards of the day on Robin. Instead, Nora is trapped in Robin's night world, a world that she does not understand. This is why Nora seeks out Matthew, who, as an inhabitant of the night like Robin, can explain both Robin and the night to her. Nora is powerless to act in the night, because action, will, and reason are all made meaningless by it. The power of the night is such that an inhabitant of the day like Nora is changed through the slightest association with it. Consequently, Nora, who once represented goodness and clarity, is now associated with evil and obscurity: it is now Nora who loves "purity's black backside."

The passage in which Nora mistakenly blamed herself for Robin's "corruption" should be read carefully, because it shows the disparity between Nora's morality of the day and the amorality of the night. Nora recalls the day that she will remember always, when she awakened Robin by striking her and thereby "corrupted" her. Robin's very identity is bound up with the idea of sleep because she is a somnambulist, or a nightwalker. This association with sleep is of course related to her association with the night. Nora remembers:

> She was asleep and I struck her awake. I saw her come awake and turn befouled before me, she who had managed in that sleep to keep whole . . . I didn't know that it was to be me who was to do the terrible thing! No rot had touched her until then, and there before my eyes I saw her corrupt all at once and withering because I had struck her sleep away, and I went mad and I've been mad ever since. (145)

The very terms of the story Nora tells—wholeness, rot, and corruption—would be meaningless to Robin. These are the judgments of morality and reason as they try and fail to make a framework for the forces of the night. Robin's sleep is not the innocent sleep of the child, as Nora makes it out to be, but a lapse into anonymity and a return to the unconscious, where the rules of the day do not apply.

Matthew's lessons on the night are not easily absorbed by Nora at this point: her identification with the day makes her a resistant student, even after she has become more knowledgeable through contact with the night. Yet the night has such extensive and subversive powers that it affects even those who are unaware of its strength, like Nora in the early stages of the novel. This is the subject of one of Matthew's earliest lessons from "Watchman, What of the Night?" in which he tries to show Nora that even the virtuous are corrupted by the night's subversive powers. According to Matthew, in sleep and in dreams we commit acts that we would never commit in the light of day. He reminds Nora that it is not

only Robin who betrays her lover in her sleep but also those who
are virtuous, like Nora herself.

> And what of our own sleep? *We go to it no better—and betray her*
> *with the very virtue of our days* . . . no sooner has our head touched
> the pillow, and our eyes left the day, than a host of merrymakers
> take and get. We wake from our doings in a deep sweat for that
> they happened in a house without an address, in a street in no
> town, citizened with people with no names with which to deny
> them. *Their very lack of identity makes them ourselves.* (88; empha-
> sis added)

In Matthew's account of the dream, identity and the proper are
effaced: there are no markers of name or place with which to identify anything. Because of this anonymity, we commit any action
we wish in a free-for-all in which repressed desires are acted upon.
The "virtue of our days" is the result of our repression of natural
vice; therefore, this virtue is the cause of the night's vice (we "betray
her with the very virtue of our days"). As Matthew vividly states:
"There is not one of us who, given an eternal incognito, a thumb-
print nowhere set against our soul, would not commit rape, mur-
der and all abominations" (88). In the anonymous world of dreams
we can act without fear of repercussions, and in the space of the
night we can act with the same freedom. The night has this effect
on all people, obliterating the distinction between those associated with the day and those associated with the night. If only in
sleep, Nora herself joins Robin, Matthew, and the other sleepwalk-
ers, who are all criminals, for they act upon their wishes. In the
novel's final chapter, "The Possessed," Nora and Robin finally
come together through a dissolution of identity: because they are
no longer opposed as representing good and evil respectively, their
union is made possible by the effects of the night.

The night world of evil, crime, and sex that Barnes explores in
Nightwood is one that few women writers have explored (Kathy
Acker joins Barnes in this). This locus is typically associated with
male writers such as the French symbolists and in this century,
Jean Genêt. For Barnes, as for Genêt, this night world's characteristic inhabitant is the homosexual, or, in the novel's terms, the
"invert." *Nightwood*'s inverts, its theories of inversion, and the

textual inversions that dramatize them both will be the focus of the remainder of the chapter, for it is by means of its figures of gender inversion that the text of *Nightwood* works to dismantle the masculine/feminine opposition.

Denaturalizing Sex and Gender

In *Nightwood*, gender is a free-floating range of possibilities: one is neither masculine nor feminine, but both masculine and feminine to varying degrees and in various combinations. This may sound like a utopian state, but that is hardly the situation sketched by the novel. When sex and gender are conceived not as fixed and certain, but as unstable and shifting—in short, variable—this situation sometimes causes conflict and pain, as it does for Robin and Matthew.[10] These characters, who typify the difficulties of those whose gender identities are compound and multiple, struggle with the culturally constructed meanings attached both to their sexed bodies and to their gender identifications. It seems at first that only their gender is mutable, but if one takes these gender permutations seriously, it is clear that their sex is mutable as well. If anatomy (or sex) is not seen as destiny, then gender need no longer be conceived as equivalent to sex; in other words, femaleness does not presuppose femininity. This allows the body to be cut loose from culturally prescribed meanings, yet this does not result in the return to a precultural, natural, and, therefore, nongendered state, for that would be impossible. Once cut loose from these prescribed meanings, newly sexed and gendered meanings may be devised for the body. Some of these new inscriptions of gender are embodied in Matthew's figures of inversion.

Several passages typify Barnes's new configurations of gender that predominate in the novel, one being Robin's experience of pregnancy. When Robin becomes pregnant early in the novel, she thinks of her pregnancy as "some lost land in herself" (*Nightwood* 45). At this point, she begins to wander far from home, a habit that becomes characteristic over the course of the novel and that underlines her similarity to animals. After giving birth, she is described as "looking about her in the bed *as if she had lost something* . . . A week out of bed *she was lost*, as if she had done something irreparable, as if this act had caught her attention for the first time" (48; emphasis added). At first, the child she is about to have is represented as "a lost land" within her, in the sense that it occupies a body that had formerly been hers entirely. Robin then experiences giving birth as the loss of "something": the "land" within her that was lost to the child (in other words, her uterus, which held the fetus) now seems doubly lost since she has given birth. This double loss is then further compounded, becoming the loss of her very self: "a week out of bed *she* was lost." The "fury" and "despair" that marked Robin's feelings about having a child lead to her "cursing like a sailor" during childbirth, an act that underscores her masculinity even during this most feminine of acts. Her despair is then transmuted into a rage that leads her to nearly kill the child (48). Threatening to dash the child to the floor is a gesture that she repeats with the doll that she gives to Nora; in the second instance, she actually does throw the doll/child to the floor. Robin's pregnancy is figured as a loss rather than as a "gift" of life, and this indicates her refusal of motherhood as an intrinsic trait of femininity and femaleness. Robin rejects the necessity of the link between motherhood and femaleness because maternity is not an expression of her gender identity. Because Robin does not possess the intrinsic femininity that is supposed to follow from her sex, even her sex is put into question. Maternity becomes a means by which Robin understands her distance from femininity.[11]

The refusal to be constrained by normative sex and gender is shared by Matthew, the novel's other invert. Inversion in Matthew's case involves a more conscious desire than in Robin's case. He wishes to be a different sex and a different gender. Since Barnes does not see anatomy as a constraint upon gender, however, Matthew can mime women and thereby become a woman in a man's body. While Robin rejects motherhood, Matthew longs for it, in an inversion of traditional gender roles that is typical of the novel.[12] Matthew often refers to himself as a girl or a woman ("am I not the girl to know of what I speak?" [90]) and bemoans the fact that although he is anatomically male, he is psychically feminine. Matthew tends to see his gender as being at odds with his sex: " '[N]o matter what I may be doing, in my heart is the wish for children and knitting. God, I never asked better than to boil some good man's potatoes and toss up a child for him every nine months by the calendar. Is it my fault that my only fireside is the outhouse?'" (91). Matthew is unable to have a home or a "fireside," which is something that he sees as a luxury attained only by those with a legitimate sexuality. His only home is the outhouse or kiosk, a place for cruising men. Matthew's desire to *be* a woman seems to follow from his desire for men. Matthew longs to have the body of a woman and a woman's capacity to reproduce, so he occasionally dresses as a woman and mimes the sex that he can never possess "naturally." Yet he feels that he is more a woman than Robin is, perhaps more a woman than any woman, as I discuss below.

Although Barnes trumps up Matthew's authority and uses him to mock the male fascination with women, his "gender trouble," to use Butler's term, is not mocked. Rather, his gender trouble actually makes his theories of the invert or "the third sex" more believable because these theories are informed by experience. Matthew feels that his love for men has been thwarted because he was born a man. He tells his tale of thwarted desire in terms of past lives:

> "In the old days I was possibly a girl in Marseilles thumping the dock with a sailor . . . am I to be blamed if I've turned up this time as I shouldn't have been, when it was a high soprano I wanted, and deep corn curls to my bum, with a womb as big as the king's kettle, and a bosom as high as the bowsprit of a fishing schooner? And what do I get but a face on me like an old child's bottom—is that a happiness, do you think?" (90–91)

Matthew's desire to be a woman who loves men rather than a man who loves men seems to indicate his wish to be able to love in a culturally intelligible and validated way. That is to say, he longs for the shelter of heterosexuality. Matthew's image of the woman he was meant to be is inflated by hyperbole: he/she would have the highest voice, the longest hair, the deepest womb, and the highest bosom. Matthew's fantasy of himself, then, exaggerates the features of stereotypical femininity. Femininity seems less natural as a result of this transvestite's image of it: drag makes evident the cultural construction of all gender roles.[13]

The shifting, unstable nature of Matthew's gender emerges clearly in his many asides on himself. In "Watchman," as a prelude to his account of the first meeting of Robin and Jenny, Matthew explains to Nora, "It was more than a boy like me (who am the last woman left in the world, though I am the bearded lady) could bear, and I went into a lather of misery watching them and thinking of you" (100). Matthew's gender is put into question the moment it is established by virtue of the way in which the subject of speech in these remarks is predicated: the "boy" underscores his undeveloped masculinity and his helplessness as a witness of this fateful meeting; the "last woman" suggests that he alone retains some vestige of true femininity compared to those who are anatomically female. Perhaps the most apt description is of himself as the "bearded lady," for he is an anomaly, a strange confusion of masculine and feminine. The thought of Nora's pain causes Matthew's misery, and his close identification with her may lead in part to his identification of himself as a woman in these remarks. In another instance where his unstable gender comes to the fore, Matthew refers to himself as "the other woman that God forgot" (143). According to him, Nora uses him as a confessor because he is the woman that God forgot, or "the girl that God forgot," as he also calls himself (73). Not only is he a woman in a man's body (and thus God has forgotten him), but he is an exceptional woman, the most womanly of women, as he establishes in the passages mentioned above. This endows him with a knowledge of the love of woman for woman, and of another special case like Robin, who may be, in a similar way, the last boy that God forgot. Just as Matthew, a man, is "the girl that God forgot" precisely in that he is a man and yet a girl, Robin is "the boy that God forgot" in that she is a woman and yet a boy. These complex formulations indicate the complexity of the relations among sex, gender, sexual practice, and desire in the novel. But if Matthew is "the girl that God forgot," what does this mean for his role as the theoretician of sexuality and gender?

The Theoretician of Sex as Bearded Lady: Dr. Matthew O'Connor

"Dr. Matthew-Mighty-grain-of-salt-Dante-O'Connor" is a theorist as well as a priest figure who hears confessions (80). As a storyteller and theorist, Matthew carries great weight in the novel, but his full title (he is "mighty" but not worth "a grain of salt") seems to suggest that he is a mockery. Matthew is a figure of masculine discursive authority in the novel, and his monologues occupy so much of the novel that he sometimes seems a second narrator. But his apparent discursive authority in the text should be questioned, not taken at face value. To question Matthew's authority is to question the masculine prerogative to know in general, and to know the truth of woman in particular. Nora approaches Matthew with questions—"What is Robin?" and "What is the love of woman for woman?"—that are versions of the age-old question, "What is woman?" Men have always attempted to answer this question (and Nora's asking these questions aligns her with the masculine), but have always "knocked their heads against it," as Freud complained ("Femininity" 113). Like Freud, Derrida, or Jardine's writers of gynesis, Matthew seeks to usurp the place of the feminine subject.[14] By questioning Matthew's apparent discursive authority, we are merely following Barnes's lead, for she has made him a mockery of the authoritative male theorist: because he longs desperately to be a woman, he envies women bitterly.

One way to question his authority in the novel is by considering his "profession"—gynecology. Many critics note that Matthew is a quack, but few find his specialty worth mentioning, though it is significant. Matthew is a gynecologist, and an "unlicensed practitioner" who practices with license at that (35). Throughout the novel, the only occasion on which he "practices medicine" is when he makes his house call on Robin in "La Somnambule," if throwing water on a woman who has fainted can be called medicine. The other references to his profession in the text are some details about his medical instruments. Matthew's oath "May my dilator burst and my speculum rust, may panic seize my index finger before I point out my man" (32) seems to have come true by the time that Nora goes to see him in his rooms in "Watchman, What of the Night?," for his tools are rusted and he, if not his index finger, is in a panic about being discovered in drag by Nora. In this passage, while Nora takes in the sight of Matthew in gown and curls, the narrator describes his surroundings, dwelling on the assortment of objects on Matthew's dresser.

> On a maple dresser . . . lay a rusty pair of forceps, a broken scal-
> pel, half a dozen odd instruments that she could not place, a
> catheter, some twenty perfume bottles, almost empty, pomades,
> creams, rouges, powder boxes and puffs. From the half-open
> drawers of this chiffonier hung laces, ribands, stockings, ladies'
> underclothing and an abdominal brace which gave the impres-
> sion that the feminine finery had suffered venery. (78–79)

The reader's shock is as great as Nora's when making this visit.
The tools of Matthew's medical arts are sure to maim any woman
who comes into contact with them: the forceps are rusty and the
scalpel broken. It is difficult not to see Matthew as a misogynist
after reading this passage. Why does the text provide this exhaus-
tive catalog of objects? First, this description provides a backdrop
for the heavily rouged man lying in bed in his nightgown. The
specific objects on the dresser are significant, however.

The description of Matthew's dresser-top is a catalog of mis-
matched objects: women's makeup bottles lie next to rusty medical instruments; lacy "ladies' underclothing" lies next to a man's
abdominal brace. Just as Matthew's sex, gender, and sexuality are
incongruent in that they form no logical, intelligible order according to prevailing norms, so is the assortment of objects in his private space incongruent. The result of this confusion of objects—
feminine/masculine, cosmetic/medical, whole/broken—is that
the privileged objects are contaminated by the very nearness of
the others. And what is privileged here is the feminine finery, for
it corresponds with the rouged and bewigged man lying in bed.
In private, Matthew plays at being a woman, and these objects
enable him to carry out his fantasy. Although the masculine objects correspond to Matthew's "real" gender and his public persona,
for Matthew these are not real but a false and yet inescapable condition. We can see this tension between the privileged feminine
objects and the loathed masculine objects in the description of the
masculine brace, whose proximity sexually taints the women's lingerie: it "gave the impression that the feminine finery had suffered
venery." Matthew's collection of feminine adornments constructs
femininity as a pose, a facade created by the application to a blank
surface (the woman) of a series of coverings: rouge, powder, perfume, hair combs, clothing, and so on. Matthew is deprived of a

"natural" femininity, yet Barnes suggests through this concept of femininity as a facade or a masquerade that femininity does not exist in a natural state. Thus, it is available to Matthew to the same degree that it is available to any woman, but Matthew clings to the idea of natural femininity.[15]

Through this description of objects, the text not only constructs femininity as a masquerade, but it also brings together Matthew's public persona and his private persona.[16] In private, Matthew plays at being a woman by donning perfume, pomade, stockings, and lace.[17] In public, on the other hand, Matthew is Dr. O'Connor, the great storyteller and unlicensed doctor. His choice of gynecology seems arbitrary until we discover that Matthew longs to be a woman, for being a gynecologist helps relieve Matthew's frustration at being a man. Since he cannot be a woman, he can at least attempt to control women by means of his authority as a doctor. Since his desire to be a woman is thwarted and impossible to realize actually, he cultivates and studies women's bodies—both their internal parts and their diseases—as well as the external finery used to adorn their bodies. But if Matthew is a quack who practices gynecology because of his envy of women, what is the result of this characterization on his position as the authority on sexuality in the novel?

Some critics see Matthew as the narrative foundation of the novel. Elizabeth Pochoda, for example, asserts that Matthew controls the novel's language, as if he, rather than Barnes, has written the novel. For this reason, she claims that the chapter entitled "The Possessed" is a stylistic failure and "anticlimax" because it is not propelled by Matthew's storytelling abilities.[18] Pochoda does not consider that Barnes has silenced him; rather, she insists that his silence *is* Barnes's silence. By displacing the female author and replacing her with a male character, Pochoda blocks a feminist reading of the gender ambiguity that Barnes has put into play in her portrayal of Matthew. Although Pochoda denies Barnes authorial control, in a gesture suggestive of the poststructuralist notion of "the death of the author," she grants it fully to Matthew. Charles Baxter also attributes the control of the novel to Matthew, suggesting that "the novelist continues to write as long as O'Connor can talk" (1177). For Alan Singer, the monologues bear such weight that he mistakenly attributes certain passages in the novel to the doctor when in fact it is the narrator speaking (75, 82). This tendency to privilege Matthew to the point of erasing the actual narrator is a common feature of the criticism written before the feminist revival of Barnes in the 1980s. In recent criticism, Matthew's ambiguous authority is noted by Jane Marcus, for example, who also sees him as a parody of Freud. Donna Gerstenberger sees his narrative power as contained by that of Barnes. She is correct to note that although his "stories often seem to exist for their own telling," they are "nonetheless inscribed within Barnes's narrative purpose" (136). In a text that does so much to undermine all hierarchies, it is difficult to maintain that a figure such as Matthew holds such overwhelming discursive authority that he usurps the actual narrator's position.

Through these details of Matthew's portrayal—his quackery, his falling silent in a drunken heap in "Go Down, Matthew," his envy of women, and his self-mockery—Barnes creates a ridiculous figure, one that evokes laughter and sympathy more than reverence.[19] Barnes trumps up his authority and undercuts it at every turn. In doing so, she inscribes a male figure who tries to usurp the feminine role, but who nevertheless holds on tight to his masculine prerogatives. When we consider that Matthew also seems to be a sketch of a nineteenth-century sexologist in his use of terms like "invert" and his constant theorizing on sexuality, this only makes the parody more biting. Through her transvestite gynecologist/priest/psychoanalyst, Barnes reveals some very interested motives behind the masculine discursive fascination with women. Matthew devises his theories of "the third sex" in order to explain Robin to Nora but also to come closer to an understanding of woman for himself. The undecidability of both the invert and the woman undermines Matthew's own authority, making him a still more ambiguous figure. Yet this ambiguity may better qualify him as an authority on subjects that by their questionable status undermine authority.

Sexual/Textual Inversions: The "Prince-Princess"

Matthew responds to Nora's questions about the night and about Robin with a series of compelling rhetorical figures for the invert, figures that operate by means of syntactical inversion. What is the

status of masculine and feminine before inversion takes place?
Barnes is writing both within and against a dominant tradition in
which discourse is organized around binary oppositions rooted
in the man/woman couple. *Nightwood* centers around a series of
privileged terms that are traditionally associated with the feminine in the history of Western culture: the night, the irrational,
and the unconscious.[20] Although the feminine is privileged rather
than the masculine, the gender binary prevails, for the hierarchy
has simply been overturned. Barnes goes further in questioning
this hierarchy, however, with her figures of inversion. Matthew
uses the term "invert" to describe a state of vacillation or a blurring and confusion of genders within the subject rather than a
simple predominance of feminine over masculine or masculine
over feminine as in a hierarchical binary structure. Since masculinity and femininity are not eradicated but proliferated through
inversion, the gender binary is at the same time assumed in these
figures and questioned and disrupted through them. Inversion
involves the figuring and refiguring of gender, for inversion consists of the presence of both genders within the subject. For example,
when female sex is joined to masculine gender identity and desire
for women, to simply name the gender of this subject "feminine"
or "masculine" is inadequate and misleading. This complex gender identity cannot be designated by these terms, yet it does not
exist outside this binary; rather, it is an offshoot of the binary.[21]
Masculine and feminine are propagated and proliferated in such
a subject, one that *Nightwood* designates variously as the third sex,
the invert, the prince, the doll, and the Sodomite.

Matthew's first theory of the origin of homosexuality is
prompted by Nora's remark about Robin's masculine appearance:
"I, who want power, chose a girl who resembles a boy" (136).
Matthew picks up this thread and weaves a tale about love for the
"same" sex, but this is clearly not love for the "same" sex, pure
and simple, for Robin's resemblance to a boy is the mark of her
difference. According to Matthew, the love for the "invert" arises
from childhood, specifically from childhood reading of romances
and fairy tales. The passage reads:

> What is this love we have for the invert, boy or girl? It was they
> who were spoken of in every romance that we ever read. *The girl*

lost, what is she but the Prince found? The Prince on the white horse that we have always been seeking. *And the pretty lad who is a girl, what but the prince-princess in point lace*—neither one and half the other, the painting on the fan! We love them for that reason. (136; emphasis added)

What we find in this discussion of inverts is a series of inversions, both syntactical and logical. The figure for female homosexuality is the prince: "the girl lost," the lesbian, is "the Prince found." And yet, "the Prince" is also the term for the male homosexual in the rest of the passage, which will be discussed below. It seems at first that the figure for the female invert is based upon the male and derived from it secondarily. This is a familiar scheme, common in Freudian theory. But when we turn to the discussion of the male invert, we find that there is no stable or primary referent in the passage whatsoever. The only referent for the male homosexual is the girl (he is "the pretty lad who is a girl"), yet the girl is the prince. The second referent for the male homosexual is the prince-princess: the male invert—"the pretty lad who is a girl"—is "the prince-princess in point lace." In other words, the figure for the male invert refers to the figure for the female invert and vice versa. There is no way out of this closed circle of reference, for we are never told exactly what "the Prince" is. This figure becomes still more mysterious in this description: "The girl lost, what is she but the Prince found? The Prince on the white horse that we have always been seeking." We have always sought the prince, for he is a desirable object, but once we find him, it is only to discover that the prince is female—he is "the girl lost." This type of young masculinity and bravado turns out to be a boyish woman in drag, and "the girl lost," when we find her, is a feminine and boyish prince. In each case, our expectations are confounded, so we must continue our search, for what we have found is not what we were looking for. This search is also endless because these fairy-tale figures are fictional and therefore elusive. We may search the world over, but we will not find them, for they imprinted themselves upon our imaginations in childhood, and this childhood realm is their only locus.

To return to the figure for the male invert: he is described early in the passage not just as the prince but as "the prince-princess."

This formulation suggests a gender ambiguity that the male invert possesses but not the female invert. This figure is adorned in "point lace," a detail that recalls Matthew's feminine finery, spilling lavishly out of his dresser drawer when Nora arrives at his room at the beginning of "Watchman, What of the Night?" Why is the gender ambiguity of the female invert apparently captured by the comparison to the prince ("the girl lost" is "the Prince found"), while that of the male invert is not adequately described by the comparison to the prince? In other words, why the asymmetry in the figures for the two inverts, while other parts of the passage suggest that inversion is inversion, regardless of the invert's sex? Matthew seems to need to use a bigendered term to convey male inversion. Although the princess enters the scheme here, she does so only in the composite figure of the "prince-princess," and she is absent from the rest of Matthew's musings. As we will see in the continuation of this passage, the invert is more prince than princess perhaps because, as an authoritative male speaker, Matthew wants to retain his masculine privilege, a privilege outside the domain of princesses.

What are the implications of the absence of the princess from the rest of the passage on the invert as prince? Perhaps the pertinent question is not why the princess is omitted later in the passage but why it is added early in the passage. The "prince-princess in point lace" may be read as an intrusion into the text of the mark of transvestism—the mark of Matthew's particular brand of inversion.[22] Just as Matthew's lacy lingerie peeks from his drawer in "Watchman, What of the Night?" further exposing him for what he is or longs to be, so this distinctly feminine image of the princess peeks through and bursts in upon his otherwise predominantly masculine figures of princes. In other words, femininity, excessive with respect to discourse according to Irigaray, shows its face here (*This Sex* 78). And this femininity is Matthew's mark—the mark of transvestism. In a sense, a transvestite who is also an invert, like Matthew, is the most overt transgressor of the gender binary. Yet if transvestism entails a transgression of the gender binary, how is it that Matthew believes he can capture femininity by means of transvestism? Matthew fails to see that because the trappings of womanhood are transferrable and may be worn on men as well as women, they do not convey stable, essential femininity, but instead they point to unstable, constructed femininity, or femininity as masquerade. Although he is well aware of the instability of gender identity and the incongruence between sex and gender in himself, Matthew regards his feminine masquerade not as the subversion of the gender binary, which it is, but as a means to capturing and claiming true femininity for himself.[23] Thus, Matthew, as a transvestite invert, is a regressive figure, for he sees himself as a woman trapped in a man's body.

Despite the one appearance of the princess, the overall emphasis of the passage is on princes. This emphasis on masculinity escalates when the princess is dropped from the rest of Matthew's musings. Matthew goes on to stress the origin of desire in childhood reading and fantasy and then, once again, defines the nature of inversion: "We were impaled in our childhood upon them as they rode through our primers, the sweetest lie of all, now come to be in boy or girl, for in the girl it is the prince, and in the boy it is the girl that makes a prince a prince—and not a man" (136–37). The basis of object choice in childhood reading shows the grounding of desire in fantasy. Barnes has chosen the sort of fairy-tale figures that usually form the basis for heterosexual fantasies. Yet the gallant prince on the white charger is not only the rescuer of Sleeping Beauty and Cinderella but also the desirable object for the male invert and the model for both the male and female invert. Matthew calls this childhood fixation on the characters of children's storybooks "the sweetest lie of all," because these characters are fictional, idealized creatures whom we seek, but never find. This love is the "sweetest" lie of all in part because Matthew is a lover of princes himself. But more importantly, this lie is "sweetest" because desire in *Nightwood* is firmly rooted in the imagination and is best kept there—desire, once realized, becomes failed love.

This passage about inversion employs a rhetorical figure based on syntactical inversion; thus, textual inversion doubles sexual inversion. The last phrase in the passage contains a chiasmus, typically a symmetrical structure, although this one is asymmetrical: "[I]n the girl it is the *prince*, and in the boy it is the *girl* that makes a prince a prince and not a *man*" (137; emphasis added).[24] If this were a symmetrical chiasmic reversal, the sentence would read: "[I]n the girl it is the *prince*, and in the boy it is the *princess*." Yet this version of the sentence is impossible, because Matthew has removed the princess from the model entirely. The reason, as noted above, is that the princess signifies not just femininity but the transvestite's version of femininity, and transvestites are a special case of inverts. Another symmetrical variation of the sentence is "[I]n the girl it is the *boy* and in the boy it is the girl." The girlish aspect of the boy makes him a prince, but the princely aspect rather than the boyish aspect of the girl makes her a prince in Matthew's version of the model.[25] The prince is also the model for the invert, male or female, for the girl and the boy are treated as one here: "[I]n the girl it is the prince, and in the boy it is the girl that makes a prince a prince and not a man." The sentence explains what causes *both* boy and girl to become princes. In other words, the female invert and the male invert are described by means of the same figure—that of the prince. Another asymmetry in the text involves the girl again. Matthew states that it is the prince in the girl and the girl in the boy that creates inversion or "makes a prince a prince and not a man." The male invert (prince) is "not a man," as stated by the text; by the same token, the female invert (prince) is not a woman. Yet the text only implies that the female invert is not a woman; it does not state it. The asymmetry here is so great that it is as if the conclusion of the sentence were lopped off: the fact that the female invert is not a woman is simply omitted from the passage. But perhaps this asymmetry is not the result of Matthew's privileging of the masculine model. Barnes may be suggesting that a female homosexual is still a woman in a way that a male homosexual cannot be a man. "Womanhood" is not threatened by homosexuality as "manhood" is, because of the historical privilege and status of the latter. The omission of the statement that the female invert is not a woman may also suggest that women have a fundamental bisexuality, as Freud argued.

Why is the male the primary referent in Matthew's discussion of the invert? There are two factors that cause the text's blind spot concerning the girl. First, a boy who is like a girl and a girl who is like a boy are essentially the same creatures, that is, ambiguously gendered, "third-sexed" creatures. Second, an androgyny where masculinity is slightly more predominant seems to be privileged in *Nightwood* by means of Matthew's focus on Robin; therefore, the prince is the predominant model, not the "prince-princess."

We see this in Robin's unself-conscious androgyny (she is "a girl who resembles a boy"), which is privileged in the novel, whereas Matthew's transvestism, which rests on a belief that he is truly a woman, makes him a parodic figure.[26] Because both male and female inverts have the same origin (in childhood fixations on androgynous characters) and because they have the same qualities (an androgyny where masculinity is slightly more pronounced and love for the same sex), Matthew uses the same term to refer to them: they are "the third sex" or "the invert." The use of the same term for female and male inverts also works to undo the binary opposition between male and female: "the third sex" questions the hierarchical opposition between the first and second sex.

The asymmetry of the syntax in the passages describing the prince is not merely an aberration of a classically symmetrical figure of speech. The symmetrical versions described above are dependent upon the diametrical or binary opposition between masculine and feminine. To posit the male and female homosexual as diametrical opposites would be in effect to recreate the masculine/feminine opposition that the text is attempting to undo by means of the figure of "the third sex." This figure is inscribed as a third term precisely in order to question the legitimacy of a strict opposition between masculine and feminine. In *Nightwood*, the masculine is inhabited by the feminine and vice versa: all of the text's inverts are not merely inverted; rather, they live out the tension between masculine and feminine and are in some way both masculine and feminine. Their state is not one of the simple inversion of gender positions, but rather of the constant vacillation between them.

Take, for example, Robin's complex gender identity. "She" is not simply a woman who, seeing herself as masculine, wants to be a man, which would imply a resolution of the conflicts between sex, gender, sexual practice, and desire. Rather, Robin is, in the terms of the novel, a girl/prince: a female (her sex), who resembles a feminine male (her gender), who is sexually involved with both men and women (her sexual practice), and who loves women (her desire). These incongruous identifications exist side by side, and the tension between them is never resolved in a simple formula such as "Robin is a man in a woman's body."[27] Robin is *not* a man in a woman's body but a woman who loves women, who seems

masculine, and whose very body and self-presentation also seem
masculine. A passage from Butler describes the kind of intricately
gendered being that Robin is:

> [I]t is possible to become a being whom neither *man* nor *woman*
> truly describes. This is not the figure of the androgyne nor some
> hypothetical "third gender," nor is it a *transcendence* of the bi-
> nary. Instead, it is an internal subversion in which the binary is
> both presupposed and proliferated to the point where it no longer
> makes sense. (*Gender Trouble* 127; emphasis in original)

Robin is indeed a being whom neither "man" nor "woman" describes
adequately, a member of "the third sex." Butler cautions her reader,
however, that the type of gendered being she describes is something other than the androgyne or the "hypothetical 'third gender.'"
While the notion of "the third sex" was first coined to describe the
idea of the man trapped in a woman's body and has also been
understood as an androgynous state beyond gender, Barnes's
"third sex" is a radical reconceptualization of this idea.[28] Her
vision of "the third sex" is much closer to contemporary notions of
the socially constructed, performative nature of gender. By means
of this third term, which would undermine the binary opposition
between masculine and feminine, Barnes's text refuses simple
binary opposition or symmetry in its articulation of gender.

"The Third Sex"

Matthew's second model for homosexuality, the doll, is similar to
the prince: it is lifeless, yet lifelike; it derives from childhood; and
its gender is ambiguous. Matthew offers his second theory in
response to Nora's story of the doll that Robin gave her. Nora
regards a doll given to a woman by her lover as a replacement for,
or a representation of, the child they cannot have: "We give death
to a child when we give it a doll—it's the effigy and the shroud;
when a woman gives it to a woman, it is the life they cannot have,
it is their child, sacred and profane" (142). As a gift from a woman
to her lover, the doll is a stand-in for the child the women cannot
have, indicating the attempt to model their life after a heterosexual

relationship, an attempt that necessarily fails. In a sense, the doll is a sign of this failure, yet Nora is nevertheless attached to the doll as a gift from Robin.[29] Thus, when Robin throws and "kills" the doll in a fit of rage, the action devastates Nora. This incident takes place when Robin returns home after wandering the night streets, a habit that underscores the distance between the lovers. Nora attributes Robin's violent treatment of the doll to the fact that "she was angry because for once I had not been there all the time, waiting" (148). For Nora, the doll is a mediator between Robin and herself: it is a replacement for the connection that is lacking between them.

The doll resembles the prince not only in its relation to child-hood fantasy, but also in the way that it is inscribed in the text: both models appear as chiasmic reversals. After discussing Robin's sense of herself as the doll, Matthew likens the doll explicitly to the invert:

> *The last doll, given to age, is the girl who should have been a boy, and the boy who should have been a girl.* The love of that last doll was foreshadowed in that love of the first. The doll and the imma-ture have something right about them, *the doll because it resembles but does not contain life, and the third sex because it contains life but resembles the doll.* (148; emphasis added)

In this passage, the origin of homosexuality is located again in childhood, or, rather, in a regression to childhood ("the last doll given to age" is the doll that an adult might give to another adult, as Robin gives Nora a doll and Felix a baby). More importantly, the "last doll" is a metaphor for the homosexual: "the girl who should have been a boy and the boy who should have been a girl." The love that they inspire was "foreshadowed" in the love of the first doll of childhood, just as the love of the prince as invert was foreshadowed, or actually inspired by, the love of the prince in fairy tales. The model for homosexuality is again a replica of a person that children endow with a name, a character, and so on, like the prince. Children may project their desires onto such figures; they may perceive them as doubles of themselves. In short, the doll and the prince can be transformed into whatever the child wants them to be because they are purely fictional. Like the doll for Nora, the prince is also a beloved yet lost object that is introjected and incorporated through melancholia. In the same way, Nora loves Robin because Robin's lack of identity at first allows her to be transformed into anything. In this sense, the doll and the invert are both inanimate figures that can be animated.

Again, the structure of the passage is that of a chiasmus—this time, a double chiasmus. The first sentence is a simple symmetrical chiasmus: "the girl who should have been a boy, and the boy who should have been a girl." The sentence beginning "the doll and the immature" forms a nearly symmetrical chiasmus: "the doll because it resembles but does not contain life, and the third sex because it contains life but resembles the doll." The structure of this figure is symmetrical; however, the final word in the passage, "doll," throws off the symmetry. Were this fully symmetrical, the end of the sentence would read, "it contains life but does not resemble it." As in the passage on the prince, the text construes sexual inversion as syntactical inversion. The symmetry of these inversions at first seems to imply a simple acceptance of a binary scheme for gender: homosexuality is the result of being misplaced in one's anatomical sex. But this simple inversion—the invert is the girl who should have been a boy and the boy who should have been a girl—is subverted by the language of the rest of the passage.

There Matthew describes the doll's face as a composite of two sexless beings: "The blessed face! It should be seen only in *profile*, otherwise it is observed to be the conjunction of the identical *cleaved halves* of sexless misgiving!" (148; emphasis added). In other words, the doll's face is neither masculine nor feminine, and for this reason in particular he uses the metaphor of the doll for the homosexual. Matthew's image relies on the idea of the splitting in two (as implied by "cleaved," "halves," and "profile") of something that we expect to be whole (the face). Yet "cleave" also refers to a joining together. The face is that part of the body traditionally thought to convey identity, a concept that implies wholeness and unity. Because the invert's face is divided and torn asunder, the only way to convey the impression of the whole (an idea that is implicit in the meaning of the face) is to look at only one half—the profile.

One word in this passage seems to work against the predominant note of division and disunity. That is "identical": the face is "observed to be the *conjunction* of the *identical* cleaved halves of sexless misgiving." Though the face of the doll/invert is divided, its parts are identical to each other. The two identical halves of the doll's face could be read as the masculine and feminine conjoined: each half consists of a blend of masculine and feminine.[30] Thus, gender confusion is not conceived as a simple case of a man trapped in a woman's body (or a woman trapped in a man's body) but as both genders inflecting one body.[31] The halves referred to in the passage are not only the parts of the face, they are also the "cleaved halves of sexless misgiving." That is, the division is caused by the uncertainty of the doll/invert about its sex, an uncertainty that results in a state of "sexless misgiving." Moreover, the sex of the invert has been "mis-given," or given wrongly: Matthew's image also implies that inversion is the result of an incorrect assignment of sex. Since the conjunction of masculine and feminine in one person is perceived as gender uncertainty in our culture, the invert seems a sexless creature, suspended in a state of uncertainty or misgiving. The text's careful delineation of the self-division of the doll/invert is what works against the seemingly simple binary scheme of these particular chiasmi. The self-division indicates that the doll/invert is made up of both masculine and feminine characteristics: so the formula "the girl who should have been a boy" then represents a girl/boy, not a boy in spirit and in sexuality who is at war with her female body.

These analogies between the invert and lifeless dolls or fairy-tale figures emphasize on one level the idea that gender and sexuality are not necessarily consistent with anatomical sex, because the connections between them are constructed through the psyche, language, and culture, and are not natural. Although homosexuality is often construed as a false miming of the "natural" genders found in heterosexuality, what Barnes is trying to get at here is the way in which "the third sex" makes explicit the performative nature of all gendered behavior.[32] A glance at a passage on "the third sex" as the "Sodomite" reveals that this is one of the reasons for the placement of the invert in the realm of the fictional as opposed to the real. In "Watchman," Matthew turns to the subject of loving a "Sodomite" after introducing the night to Nora.

"And do I know my Sodomites?" the doctor said unhappily, "and
what the heart goes bang up against if it loves one of them, especially if it's a woman loving one of them. What do they find
then, that *this lover has committed the unpardonable error of not being able to exist—and they come down with a dummy in their arms.*"
(93; emphasis added)

Although the term "Sodomite" historically refers to male inverts,
Matthew is clearly using it to refer to female inverts as well, since
he speaks of what happens when a woman loves one of them, and
Nora clearly loves a female invert. Just as he merges male and
female homosexuals under the names "prince" and "invert," so
he uses the masculine term "Sodomite" to refer to both sexes. While
Matthew's aim in describing the prince and the doll was theoretical, his aim in describing the Sodomite here is existential. The doll
and the prince were devised to show the origin of homosexuality
in childhood and to describe the qualities of this other sexuality.
These figures were also devised in order to theorize the complex
gender identity of the invert. Here, however, he explains to Nora
what *happens* when one loves a Sodomite. He speaks, that is, of his
painful experience: "And do I know my Sodomites?" refers not to
his encyclopedic knowledge of the species "invert" but to the basis for his knowledge, his own life as an invert and his frustrated
desires. His subject, as he goes on to say, is "what the heart goes
bang up against if it loves one of them."

    The invert's inability to exist causes pain and anguish to those
who love inverts. But why does Matthew claim that the invert is
"not able to exist"? Once again, the novel likens the invert or
"Sodomite" to that which is lifeless, in this case, a "dummy," which,
like the doll, is an imitation of life. Matthew's prince, similarly,
was "a lie," or a desirable object that was always sought but never
found, because it did not exist in reality. Although the prince
exists, at least in the imagination, he/she is unattainable because
he/she is not real. But the lifelessness of the Sodomite as dummy
seems more dramatic than that of the prince or the doll: the doll
"does not contain life" according to Matthew, while the Sodomite
is *"not able to exist."* The invert's habitat is the night, and consequently the invert is associated with the novel's central terms—
the anonymous, the unconscious, nonreason—which are associated

with death and nothingness. For this reason, in part, the invert "is not able to exist." The invert is also one of the many abject, outcast characters that populate this novel.[33] The invert, like other oppressed people, or other "others," lives on the margins of society, which is figured as the night in this novel, a space that is privileged, yet still marked as outside. In other words, because "the third sex" subverts binary oppositions by being a conjunction of masculine and feminine, it challenges the structure of binary opposition that shores up the world of the day, discourse, and structures of power, and is not recognizable, or "does not exist," in these contexts.

"There Is No Truth" of Gender

In attempting to resolve the question of the degree to which *Nightwood*'s figures of inversion rely upon the gender binary even as they deconstruct the truth of inversion, I will close by considering a remark of Matthew's that may be read as a self-reflexive comment on his own status as a speaker. Matthew describes to Nora the mistake involved in imposing a formula on love: "There is no truth, and you have set it between you; you have been unwise enough to make a formula; you have dressed the unknowable in the garments of the known" (136). In order to understand her love for Robin, Nora went to Matthew for an explanation of the truth about Robin, the truth about homosexuality, and the truth about the night. But these truths or formulae do not exist, and this is something that Matthew has also tried to teach Nora. Although Matthew's voice in the novel is endowed with authority, his authority is also ambiguous: while admitting that there is no truth and that he only tells lies, he nevertheless presents Nora with several accounts of inversion that sound like attempts to speak the truth. Yet rather than reveal the truth, as Matthew set out to do, he has only revealed the inadequacy of his own formulae.

While focusing on Nora's desire for the truth, this remark of Matthew's is also self-reflexive in that he is aware that he himself has "dressed the unknowable in the garments of the known." As a self-professed theorist of sexuality, Matthew has devised models for the invert that do precisely this: they take an unknowable entity

and explain it by means of familiar terms that the invert seriously
puts into question. Matthew has taken the person whose gender
is an indeterminable amalgamation of masculinity and femininity and given it a name (or several names), an origin, and a history. But for Barnes "the third sex" is fundamentally undecidable,
and any attempt to formulate it is bound to miss its mark. The
characters Robin and Matthew, as well as Matthew's theories of
the invert, have shown that masculine and feminine are not easily
distinguishable, do not neatly coincide with male and female, and
that gender is not a simple choice between two options. Although
Nightwood has ventured a theory of "the third sex," it undoes its
own attempt precisely to show that there is no certain truth of
either inversion or gender. "The third sex" is the mark of this uncertainty.

Matthew's metaphor of "dressing the unknowable in the garments of the known," as formulaic as it may seem, brings together
all the uncertainty and undecidability surrounding gender in this
text. First, it is a self-conscious remark in that it refers to his own
transvestism in an almost literal way. Although Matthew claims
that it is an error to "dress the unknowable in the garments of the
known," isn't this what he himself attempts to do by means of his
transvestism? In his desire to be a woman, he takes the costumes
and cosmetics that are cultural markers of femininity, or "the garments of the known," and uses them to "dress the unknowable."
But is the unknowable in this instance the woman Matthew longs
to be or the ambiguous gender that he possesses? In his eagerness
to be a true woman, or a woman in truth, Matthew has mistaken
the feminine masquerade for the essence of woman. Removing
the "garments" of femininity from Matthew would simply reveal
an aging man, not the beautiful young woman he longs to be. In a
similar way, his ambiguous gender, "the third sex," is unknowable (in the sense of being indeterminate and in flux) and
undecidable, and no garment could ever take the shape of its
strange contours. The text seems to suggest, then, that "the third
sex" is fundamentally "unknowable." Although the text also represents the feminine via Robin as mysterious, enigmatic, and
unknowable—in other words, as the essential feminine—it also
moves toward a recognition of femininity as a construct or masquerade. The scene in which Nora finds Matthew in drag, sur-

rounded by "feminine finery," indicates the impulse in the text toward this other view of transvestism: instead of garments failing to convey the truth of woman, garments—the masquerade—themselves constitute femininity. In this sense, Matthew may be read as both a parody of the nineteenth-century sexologist and as a prescient sketch of the contemporary gender theorist. While *Nightwood* anticipates the theorization of gender as performance, there still lingers in this rich text a belief in an essential, fundamental gender difference lurking beneath, as it were, the garments of culturally constructed, multiple gender differences.

FOUR

"A SECRET SECOND TONGUE"
The Enigma of the Feminine
in Marianne Hauser's The Talking Room

But oh, the Grecian mouth was that of a god, with the lower
lip slowly curling inside out like a secret second tongue.
—Marianne Hauser, *The Talking Room*

The enigma of woman would largely reside in the enigma
of her lips and all they keep unmanifested.
—Luce Irigaray, *Sexes and Genealogies*

B, the first-person narrator of *The Talking Room*, is preoccupied with
the oral, and this is a largely feminine preoccupation.[1] That is, her
fascination with mouths is directed at women's mouths, including her own, and, as the epigraph from Irigaray suggests, there is
an intimate connection between the feminine and the mouth. One
woman's mouth in particular draws B's attention, as well as that
of other characters: the mouth of her mother, J, which is described
in the first epigraph to this chapter. J's lover, V, was first attracted
to J because of her beautiful mouth, the "mouth of a god," which
consists of an unusual and distinct feature—her lower lip appears
to form a second tongue. J's mysterious and beautiful mouth is
only the more mysterious and beautiful because it is a silent mouth.
J rarely speaks, and when she does, her speech is enigmatic and
mysterious, merely enhancing the effect of her characteristic silence.
The text's orality is also centered in B, who loves both food and
her large body that results from her love of food. While J represents the silent feminine, B represents the verbose feminine—the
fat lady who never stops talking but whose speech is meaningless. Hauser pairs two classic and opposed images of the relation
between women and speech, but she reinscribes their meanings
by suggesting that they exist for each other rather than for the
masculine. For B centers her narrative around J and she seeks to

fill in J's blankness. The novel is a love letter from B to J, daughter to mother, woman to woman. Yet B's attachment to J surpasses the verbal; her love for her mother escapes the confines of daughterly love and spills over into eroticism. B uses her narrative to recreate J—to replace her characteristic absence with presence. In this way, B's narrative of abundant words is far from meaningless, just as J's silence signifies the presence of undefined meaning rather than the absence of meaning.

The novel's fascination with the feminine's resistance to containment and definition extends to gender and sexual identities in general, which similarly resist containment. Identity is conceived here as a space of future possibilities, with gender identity in particular being freed from the narrow constraints of the gender binary. Gender identity is conceived as multiple, fluid, and changeable. Through the depiction of J and V's butch-femme role playing, gender is constructed as performative rather than as natural. Moreover, sexual desire is as fluid and flexible as gender identity. J, for example, is both masculine and feminine, and her desire is best described as bisexual. Another boundary crosser is B, who is in love with three very different people: Olli, an adolescent boy; Uncle D, a gay male friend of V's; and her mother.

The mouth is only one of many figures for the feminine that permeate the novel. In its attempt to articulate the feminine, the novel might be said to stutter and repeat itself because of the feminine's logic-defying nature. Variously represented through the mouth, the lips, the tongue, the belly, the angel, rain, water, and the circle, the feminine appears and reappears in this text in such a way that the reader's attention is constantly drawn to it and yet deflected from it. For the text never definitively depicts or defines the feminine, instead deferring definition in favor of a view of the feminine as enigma—as full with meaning yet confounding determinate meaning.

"The Voices in the Talking Room Go Dead": B and her Mothers

The Talking Room could be categorized as a lesbian postmodern coming-of-age story. Because the novel is relatively unfamiliar to most readers, I will provide a brief description of the characters and happenings (in place of "plot") of the novel. B, the thirteen-year-old narrator, lives with her biological mother, J, and J's lover, V (whom B calls Aunt V), in lower Manhattan.[2] In her story, B focuses on the tumultuous relationship between her two mothers. J leaves periodically on drunken binges and gives no account of her whereabouts when she returns. V and B weather these frequent absences as well as J's violent behavior when she is at home. The narrative takes place in four main settings: V's house, where B centers her stories of her birth and V's and J's relationship (1–72); V's second home, "Sappho's Silo," where B focuses on her relationships with her grandmother and her boyfriend (72–102); Manhattan, especially Central Park, where B spends an afternoon with Uncle D (103–28); and, again, V's house, where the focus returns to B, V, and J (128–56). B returns again and again to the same subjects in her story: her longing for her ever-absent mother; her mother's and her own pregnancies; V's and J's relationship; and her own burgeoning sexuality.

The dynamics of the relationships among the three main characters are fascinating in and of themselves, but exploring them will also provide some basis for the further exploration of the feminine and gender that is the focus of this chapter. One component of these dynamics is the very different ways in which B, J, and V use language and narrative. Each character seems to represent a different relationship to language, which mirrors her relationship to the world.

V is the most worldly of the three and the most literal in her use of language. She provides the structure of both B's and J's existence. She is the breadwinner through her work in real estate and she owns the house in which they live. She tries to make a "normal family life" for them by periodically suggesting that J marry a man who will serve as a surrogate father for B (27).[3] She tries to rein in J's excessive drinking and her sexuality, and she does the same with B's excessive eating (35). V and J are unaware of B's sexual activity, and B fears that V would exert control over this as well. V's plans to control J went so far that having a baby was conceived as a project to tie J down: "A child will keep you from drifting. You need an anchor" (3). V is a devoted believer in the powers of psychotherapy, thinking that talk will get her to the

origin of her problems. She consults her therapist about J, and he
recommends that she devise a list of potential cures for J's wandering tendencies, which are referred to as "ideas for J-keeping"
(62). But all of V's attempts at establishing order are either paro-
died or undercut by the text. For example, when V tells B about
the various problems she is having with J, who won't stop drinking and who beats her, she suddenly becomes conscious that she
is telling a thirteen-year-old and defends herself: "I don't mind
telling this to you or anyone else. Our . . . therapist has urged us to
let everything come out. Talk, talk, no matter who listens . . .
Remove the stopper and let the juice gush out" (20). As V goes on
talking and reviewing her past as she always does, B mocks her
by punctuating V's narrative with the snide remark, "[P]ull out
that stopper!" (20). Although B pulls out her own stopper as well—
her narrative's associational structure is a freeing up of speech—
the causes and effects of her excessive talk are very different. V
endlessly reviews the past with an aim of understanding it and
also congratulating herself on her accomplishments: her stories
frequently involve accounts of her struggles and her brave sur-
mounting of obstacles.[4] She talks with a purpose, the purpose of
self-expression. B, by contrast, talks simply in order to talk. Her
speech exists for its own sake. And although she begins her narrative with an attempt to find her origin (the type of conventional
narrative that V would endorse), she abandons this attempt and
moves on to fill her narrative with accounts of daily events, such as
a trip to her grandmother's house in the country or a trip to the zoo
with Uncle D, which are punctuated by random overheard speech.

   A passage that sums up the difference between B and V in
terms of their relationships to language involves an associational
word game that they play:

> O, I said into the mirror, addressing my baby, and Aunt V re-
> sponded with Oregano . . . I said Orgy and she said Order. Then
> I really socked it to her with Offals, Orgasm, Opium, and Ova-
> ries. Dear me, she said, you're getting too smart for me, Overkill
> and Oedipus is all I can come up with . . . (154)

Using the O as a Rorschach test, V and B reveal some profound
differences. V's associations are either common and ordinary

(oregano), or suggestive of authority (order, Oedipus), or descriptive of herself (overkill). Overkill captures V's emotional and narrative style. She goes overboard to make her points; she dramatizes the slightest incident from her life. B, on the other hand, has her mind on sex, death, drugs, and the female body. B's O-words show her attraction to excess, abandon, and obliteration;[5] V's show her reliance upon external authority.

While V represents narrative as order, unity, logic, and containment, J represents the antithesis of narrative itself, the fragment. This contrast stands out most clearly when V demands that J account for her whereabouts during her long absences from the house. Upon J's return from one such absence, V demands of her "an itemized account of reality" (142), specifically the names of those she has slept with while gone. But J cannot remember anything but fragments and disconnected images of her wanderings:

> Mom would shake her head and say that she couldn't after all be sure that she hadn't dreamed it. For in the wake of her long absences, fragments of reality, dogs, bottles, men, women, beds, would briefly be washed ashore only to be swallowed up again by another dream wave and she could be sure of nothing. (142)[6]

J isn't even sure of the origin of her thoughts: like B, who is uncertain whether she dreams or overhears the talking room stories, J is uncertain whether she has lived these events or dreamed them. Just as J's grip on "reality" and the representation of it through accounting for it in a story are very tenuous, so is her identity.

The issue of J's blankness needs to be taken quite literally. J's hazy memory threatens her sense of identity. She can no more conjure up a sense of who she is than she can piece together what she has done and with whom. B describes her upon one return home in this way:

> Ghostlike, mom passes through the mirrors as though through a blizzard, staring into each mirror in search of that lost face or moment Aunt V so desperately wants her to catch and nail down. But there is nothing in the mirror to help mom remember and *she may not even recognize her own face, may stare into a void,* blankly or scared because of that big hole in her memory. (144; emphasis added)

Someone or something has come home, but it doesn't appear to be J. Since V and B have been longing for her return, it is ironic that when she does return, she is almost invisible, even to herself. Her identity has always been hazy, but here her very physical presence becomes questionable as when Hauser writes that she is "transparent as a shadow (sliding through closed doors and walls . . .)" (143). This underscores the fact that J has always been more absent than present: during another disappearance, B remarks, "mom . . . has disappeared again, though Flo says, how could she when she never was here anyhow?" (51). It is possible that we should take these remarks literally: perhaps J is not simply emotionally absent but literally absent. B and V could be tricking themselves again, since they have already used a substitute J (J2) in the "real" J's absence (129–30). J may not exist; B may be fabricating all the stories of herself and her mothers. *The Talking Room* seems to take quite literally its own status as a fictional, nonrealist text, and it reminds the reader of this status quite frequently.[7]

"My Own Big Belly": B as "Fat Lady"

B is a conspicuous presence in her own story, both physically and verbally, and these two registers mirror each other. Her large size, to which she frequently alludes, creates a powerful physical presence; her love of words and her skill at manipulating them despite her relative youth (she is only thirteen) create a powerful verbal presence. The stylistic features of B's narrative mark it as postmodern: her use of repetition and punning, her overall attention to surface and style, and her appropriation of ready-made stories and images.

The nature of "B's story," which is composed of many stories that are not "hers," makes it problematic to define this story as "hers" to begin with. B makes "her" story, *The Talking Room*, out of already existing stories, primarily ones about J and V's relationship and about her place in that relationship. The narrative thus subverts the notion of the original, as well as the notion of origin itself, since one of B's aims in the story is to uncover her origin. This is a would-be story of origin that sifts through other stories in search of an origin that is never found.[8] This story, then, must be secondhand: it is not "original." The "talking room" is the site of production for these stories: V and J talk, argue, and make up in the living room, which B renames as the talking room since living is defined by talking in this novel. She listens through her bedroom wall, constantly eavesdropping on the two women ("Mom's voice comes pushing through the night, up from the talking room" [46]). She even admits at several points that she may have made up the stories she claims to have overheard: "The voices in the talking room go dead . . . maybe I invented them in any case. Those voices, I can turn them up or down like the pocket transistor I keep going under my pillow" (2). The result of building her story upon the stories of others, which works as a kind of narrative recycling, is that her narrative has the form of a pastiche, a collage of fragments.

The novel is not only composed of ready-made stories, but it also merges B's words with found words, primarily lines from radio broadcasts. These radio announcements, generally ads and news, punctuate her narrative from beginning to end, as B seems to transcribe these from her transistor radio. She sometimes inserts the words from the radio, seemingly as is, into her story, but she also alters them to merge with her thematic or stylistic interest of the moment. After describing J's "book of unwritten poems" with the line copied from Rilke—"JEDER ENGEL IST SCHRECK-LICH"—B writes: "SHRECKS READYMADE PICKMEUP CAKEMIX FOR PROCESSED ANGELS. But the transistor under my pillow is dead and I must have tuned in on a dream" (68). B filters Rilke through the language of capitalism—advertising—in a typically postmodern merging of "low" and "high" culture. B also casts doubt on the origin of this line. It appears from outside her mind, yet her radio is dead, so it must be a dream. The ad is presented as emerging from her transistor, not her: it is as if, in an uncanny way, the radio "knows" what's going on in the novel and mirrors it. The uncertainty about the origin of these "intrusions" points to B's control over her narrative, and suggests as well that she may indeed have fabricated each supposedly overheard scene that takes place in the talking room.

The tenses of B's narration are as unusual and telling as many of its other features. Many scenes are narrated in the present tense, as if B is recording and responding to events as they occur. This places the reader in B's position: we watch and listen with her as she watches and listens to V and J. Less often, B uses the simple past typical of conventional narrative. What is most unusual, however, is her use of "might" and "would" to signal that she is describing habitual, repeated actions. Many of the scenes involving J's and V's interactions, particularly their behavior upon J's returns, are narrated in this way.[9] This unusual feature—and the almost monotonous repetition of "might" and "would" in these passages—underscores the sheer predictability of certain events in their lives. One principle of conventional narrative is surprise, the privileging of the unpredictable. Hauser seems to reject this notion and instead build her narrative around what is known because it has happened before. This creates an interesting paradox when it is compared with another feature of the narrative—B's uncertainty about so many things. Typically, her knowledge is far surpassed by her lack of knowledge. How was she conceived? Is her mother home? When will her mother return? Will she return at all? These unanswered questions plague both B and her narrative. So, when B narrates an often repeated scene, the repetition is a way for her to comfort herself with the knowledge that she does indeed know something that has happened and she knows it will most likely happen again. In the face of so much uncertainty and unpredictability, B's narrative compulsion to repeat makes a kind of emotional as well as narrative sense.

Repetition also structures the narrative on another level: in place of plot and externally imposed divisions like chapters, the novel's scenes are related through repetition on the level of the word. These repetitions are sometimes motivated by meaning and sometimes by the sound properties of words. A characteristic associative slide is found in a passage where V describes dreaming of her late husband's "you know what" (37). J bluntly fills in the demure V's blank, which closes the section: "Jock's cock. Go succotash, says mom. Wet dreams are not for nice little ladies" (38). B then repeats several of J's words as she opens the next section: "Jock, Jake or Joke. I make my own wet dreams" (38). "Jock" suggests "Jake," V's other ex, and the alteration of one letter makes a "Joke" of "Jake." Indeed, that all of V's X's are J's does seem like a joke—for example, V can regard their gifts to her, which are marked "from J," as coming from her J of the moment. As if V's interest in male genitalia ("Jock's cock," as J puts it) is suggestive, B then thinks of her "own wet dreams," her own desire. This passage demonstrates that B's narrative is structured by randomness, not so-called logical order.

Through the puns in this passage (J's "go succotash"), the emphasis is placed on the signified rather than the signifier. B puns and rhymes constantly, playing with words as if they were toys. When she tells her boyfriend Olli that she is pregnant, her language is particularly dense, made up of alliteration, assonance, and puns. In this passage, she is inspired more by the sound associations of words than their meanings. In response to Olli's dumbfounded "WHAT?" after she has told him of being pregnant in a straightforward fashion, she reverts to rhyming and punning. The lack of punctuation (including quotations marks to indicate dialogue) places emphasis on the properties of individual words rather than on the syntax and semantics of the sentence: "A cuddly fuzzy olli dolli baby bear that's what . . . I mean gee B gee whizz I mean you kiddin! Cross my womb and hope to fly" (96). B's relationship to language allies her with J, whose speech resonates like poetry, as against V, who is a literalist in respect to language, just as she is an essentialist in respect to gender.

B's orality is a thematic thread in the novel with her frequent references to her large body and her incessant eating. Both language and food are B's playthings: her orality is a love of language as much as it is a love of food. She ingests and digests words as if they were food, rolling syllables about on her tongue. But her orality also raises the question of lesbian sexuality and narrative on a textual level, given the recurring images of lips and mouths that appear throughout B's narrative. Eating is a sensual experience for B, which can be seen in her descriptions of food: "[B]uy me a psychedelic ice cream concoction drowned in fudge. Triple portions of hi ho calorie jumbo thrill melts in the mouth 9 different flavors" (112). This descriptive word pile shows B's excitement at the thought of eating such a "hi ho calorie" treat: she uses stylistic excess to mirror caloric excess, and the "thrill" she feels is matched by the energy of her description. The thrill is intensified by the fact that V forbids such excesses, causing B to wryly remark to D (who has bought her the ice cream), "O no we won't tell Aunt V" (112). Not only does V attempt to strictly monitor B's eating, but she also attempts to monitor J's equally excessive drinking. B makes explicit the link between her eating and J's drinking, which could be fodder for V's therapist, if B and J were willing: "Her therapist is itching to treat me but I won't let him. I prefer to stuff myself. I knock myself out with goodies the way mom does with booze, and he'd be more than glad to treat her too" (35). Eating is thus a link between B and her mother: they are united through excess, orality, and rebellion.

As a result of the pleasure she takes in eating, B is large; her body, particularly her belly, is expansive. But B enjoys her size, frequently referring proudly to her large belly. Rather than hiding her big body, as V encourages her to do, B flaunts it and enjoys it. As she gets ready for her big date with Uncle D, B primps and preens:

> I . . . dress to kill in . . . the white tent dress with the red poppies. No panty girdle, not for me, Aunt V, no underpants . . . Now I am free and light as air. My breasts swing loose, my hair streams bright, my belly weighs less than nothing. (109)

By reveling in her body's bigness, B eradicates the burden that her abundant flesh could represent: as she says, her "belly weighs less than nothing." For B, to be fat is to be powerful. When B climbs on top of a rock in Central Park, she enjoys her size: "I was bigger than the city, the windy skyscrapers moon sail cloud rakers that were surging over the horizon of rocks and trees" (122). Such moments of linguistic excess—the pile of nouns, the hyperbole of the comparison, the half-rhyme—are extensions of B's bodily excess. B's narrative style is as expansive and abundant as her flesh, which is another way in which the novel's postmodernism is reflected in its depiction of the feminine. Being fat also gives B command over herself in the sense that she uses it to literally expand her territory: B takes up a substantial amount of space and occupies it proudly. Her expansive body results in an expansive identity and these match the expansiveness of her language and her storytelling.[10]

B is a literal "fat lady," due to her large body size. But she is also a literary "fat lady," a figure analyzed by Patricia Parker in her *Literary Fat Ladies: Rhetoric, Gender, Property*. Parker examines the relation between the figure of the large woman and the rhetorical style of "dilatio," in which plots are slowed down and opened out (19): in other words, the fat lady uses language in an unrestrained way. *The Talking Room*'s recurrent figures of mouths and bellies situate the novel within the dilatory tradition where tongues and wombs figure as signs of dilation and copious speech (Parker 21). B's narrative takes its time developing—she unfolds no clear plot. B narrates not in order to tell *a story*, but in order to tell *stories*, to produce signs for the sake of producing signs. The closest things to a plot in this novel are the stories of B's pregnancy and of J's constant departures and returns, both of which are examples of dilation.[11] Pregnancy allows for delay and also for expansion on both literal and figurative levels: as B's body swells with pregnancy, she has yet another topic on which to dwell in her narrative. The pregnancy plot "thickens" toward the end of the novel, when B attempts to keep her pregnancy a secret from V. B fears that V will force her to have an abortion, which would rob B of the future child whom she already loves, as well as rob her story of one of its productive sidelines. Like B's pregnancy, J's wanderings are a way of providing narrative detours and delays. While B waits for J to return, she must fill out her narrative, yet she also fills her narrative with stories of J's frequent departures and returns.

The Talking Room extends the fat lady tradition in its equation of feminine speech with fullness and multiplicity of meaning rather than with emptiness and meaninglessness. Parker notes the connection between feminine lack and meaningless speech in the fat lady tradition: "If 'few words' are valued as 'good words,' then the feminine mouth which produces by contrast a throng of words is the kind of copiousness produced by this 'nothing,' the copious 'O' produced by that female deficiency or lack" (30). In this novel, the "O" signifies fullness, not lack, a plenitude of potential meanings, as in the passage in which V and B use the O as a Rorschach test, rather than the absence of meaning,. The O also represents narrative expansion and repetition rather than narrative linearity and closure. According to Parker, the eventual closure of dilatory texts is an attempt to control feminine speech. In the same way, the fat lady's pregnancy, when it comes to issue, is a way of submitting women to the patriarchal economy (26). But *The Talking*

Room resists such closure. B "ends" her story before she gives birth; thus, there is no closure on her pregnancy plot. B further resists closure in her story by ending on a scene of reunion between V and J, which, given the rest of the novel and the constant recurrence of just such scenes, seems anything but final. The last words of the novel are "around and around" (156), implying that one meaning of the O in this text is narrative circularity: the plot of V's and J's relationship has the potential to pick up and begin again.

"A Secret Second Tongue": The Enigma of the Lips

Any reference to lesbian desire in the novel seems to be connected to women's mouths in one way or another. V recalls that what drew her to J that first night at BANGS, the local lesbian bar, was her beautiful mouth, which stood out from her otherwise unappealing body: "Ragged fingernails. A hacking cough. Sallow skin. But oh, the Grecian mouth was that of a god, with the lower lip slowly curling inside out like a *secret second tongue*" (57; emphasis added). J's mouth is sensual and inviting: her lower lip acts as a border between inner and outer—it is both lip, defining the contours of the mouth, and tongue, contained within the mouth. It thus confuses the distinction between the inside and outside of the mouth. This confusion is repeated in the configuration of this secret second tongue, which is "curl[ed] inside out." This undermining of the inside/outside opposition is one aspect of the female body's two sets of lips as celebrated by Irigaray in "When Our Lips Speak Together": "[T]he passage from the inside out, from the outside in, the passage between us, is limitless. Without end. No knot or loop, no mouth ever stops our exchanges" (*This Sex* 210).[12] Irigaray's comments seem to describe not only J's mouth but also the narrative of *The Talking Room* itself: it too appears to be "limitless" and "without end."

What to make of the secretness of this "second tongue"? It appears to be secret in the sense that it is not readily apparent or readily visible, and, in this way, it is marked as lesbian.[13] V, in her desire for this mouth, sees the lip as forming another tongue. Its secretness may lie in the fact that it is not there for all to see: it takes a particularly lesbian perspective, informed by a specifically lesbian desire, to perceive this "secret second tongue."[14] The secretness of this tongue connects it to other parts of the woman's body as represented in this text. B describes her large belly as a secret space that may conceal a fetus; similarly, a beautiful mouth like J's may conceal "a secret second tongue." This one secret of the narrative may be Hauser's wry concession to the privileging of the secret in conventional narrative: but Hauser removes the secret from the domain of plot, as in the phrase "plot secret," and shifts it to the domain of the body. The feminine body may contain secrets that we cannot even see or know unless we see this body from the perspective of the desiring lesbian subject. It is this different, lesbian way of seeing, which involves the capacity to see what is secret, that actually constructs the lesbian body.

The fact that J possesses a "second" tongue is as significant as the fact that it is "secret." By doubling an organ that seems necessarily singular, is Hauser suggesting that her text is a postmodern Babel, a text that breaks down and speaks in tongues? Why would J, who is so silent throughout the novel, possess not one tongue but two? If any character would be a likely candidate for double tongues, it would seem to be B, who eats and talks so much. The second tongue may be read not as proper to J but as proper to a subjectivity defined as possessing the multiple genders and multiple sexualities that J represents in the text. This type of subject is at least bilingual, if not multilingual, for our standard frame of reference is not adequate to describe such a gender identity, as I discuss below. This bilingualism may also be a reference to the other set of lips on the female body: the lips always refer both to the mouth and to the genitals, as Irigaray has argued. These double lips suggests that labial pleasure is multiple and that the production of speech is mirrored and reaffirmed through the lips of the sex. For Irigaray, the two sets of lips on the feminine body create a multiplicity of voices for women, between women. Her reference to "several ways of speaking [that] resound endlessly" sounds like a description of Hauser's open-ended narrative style (209). Far from being silent, as woman is often signified in dominant systems of representation, women not only speak but have "several ways of speaking"—a multitude of voices, like the voices of J and V that B hears resounding in "the talking room," and to which she adds her own voice(s).

Just as V's desire for J was initially aroused by the beauty of her mouth's "secret second tongue," so B's desire for J focuses on her mouth. In a passage where B situates herself as the voyeur to V and J's lovemaking, B focuses attention on J's mouth. As V and J stand nude before the "triple mirror," V gives J an opal ring.

> My angel, [V] whispered. And she slipped the ring with the milky opal off her little finger and pressed it like a seal between her angel's thighs.
>
> 3 V's on their knees. 3 J's erect like three slim columns—*thighs locked, lips opened wide.* 3 milky opals peering through brown seaweeds.
>
> With this ring, Aunt V intones. And she slips it on mom's little finger . . . (59; emphasis added)

When V presses the "milky opal" between J's thighs, the language of the passage refers not only to the literal ring, but undoubtedly to another milky opal between a woman's thighs—the clitoris.[15] Although J's thighs are "locked," her lips are "opened wide": the lips of the mouth are referred to, but the "other" lips—the labia—are unmistakably suggested as well. Yet the language of the passage seems to resist such a slide due to the *"locked"* thighs, which would not prevent the labia from opening wide, although they would prevent B or the reader from being able to see if they were opened or shut. The mention of lips is important here, for it draws attention to J's mouth both as an object of erotic fascination and as a site of potential speech. As J's lips "open wide," her mouth becomes the sign of her desire, her clitoral pleasure (the "milkiness" of the opal/clitoris being a further sign of arousal and pleasure). Although J is characteristically silent, here her lips open wide, suggesting, if not producing, speech, just as her "secret second tongue" suggests speech. In this passage, the transgressive lesbian desire of V and J is surpassed by B, who desires her own mother. Once again, to cross one boundary is never enough for Hauser. Her transgressions multiply indefinitely, as with her breaking of one gender and sexual taboo after another.

B's sublimated desire for J emerges again when B finds the "milky opal," which J had lost, in a "trash can in the street" (61). B describes the found object in this way: "[I]t is tiny, the opal is no bigger than an apple seed. Yet what fire! I lick it till it shines and watch the tiny flames wriggle and leap" (61).[16] The stone's "fire" refers both to the type of opal it may be as well as to the "fire" it incites in B as an image of the clitoris, which is an image of lesbian pleasure. By licking the opal that is the sign of J's sex, B expresses both her desire for J and her intended effect, which is to incite J's desire in turn by making "the tiny flames wriggle and leap." Licking the opal is also another way of incorporating J through the incorporation of her image.[17]

V is drawn to the sight of women's mouths other than J's, and her ability to perceive the woman's body differently extends to these other women. When she witnesses the revelation of another woman's tongue, she is strongly affected by it as well. In a strange scene, Flo, V's African American maid, exposes her open mouth and tongue to V and B moments after V has brought up the subject of B's craving for food and the question of how she and Flo might control this in B. Flo's distance and difference from V is emphasized in the prelude to this passage when B describes her as "immensely black in her white uniform in the white kitchen" and surrounded by her white employers (36).[18] Instead of replying to V's remarks about B's excessive eating, Flo fixes V with her eyes and begins to lick her lips slowly and methodically. Both V and B are mesmerized by the sight. Here is Flo's performance: "She never blinks, she opens her mouth and moves her tongue very slowly in a wide circle over her wide lips. I see . . . how *Flo's tongue keeps sweeping around and around* while she continues to watch Aunt V" (36; emphasis added). Is Flo performing B's oral desires for V to see? Is Flo in some way challenging V? Is she trying to hypnotize her, which is one effect of her actions? Flo provides ironic commentary on V and J throughout the novel: here she may be in one sense acting out her view of the strange women who employ her. By describing Flo's tongue as "sweeping around and around," Hauser creates another image of the O and another image of endless repetition without beginning or end. In addition to being mesmerized, V also mimics her, although she is unconscious of her mimicry: "Aunt V stands as though hypnotized, with . . . her eyes held fast by Flo's eyes. Then she too opens her mouth and her tongue comes darting out of it like a gray mouse to sweep, like Flo's tongue, in that same slow circle over the thin painted lips" (36). Perhaps revealing one's mouth, like revealing one's sex, is a form of exhibitionism. If this is the case, then Flo's exhibitionist gesture inspires V to do the same. While Flo and V reveal their mouths/their sexes, B looks on, ever the voyeur or spectator, hypnotized by V's performance just as V was hypnotized by Flo's: "I stare. I too am hypnotized" (36).

When the spell is broken by the striking of the clock, V is horrified at what has just gone on: "Really! This is obscene! Aunt V cries out. Her face is blotched. Her mouth is gray. Obscene! she cries . . ." (37). The shame that V evidently feels after licking her lips in imitation of Flo is enough to suggest that she has indeed revealed something sexual, as does her censoring cry of "obscene."[19] After coming out of her trance, V loses control. But when Flo, whose "face is a blank mask" after these exchanged performances, acts "as if nothing has happened" (57), V pretends that what is "obscene" is B's excessive eating, the subject of conversation that initially led to Flo's performance. It is interesting that Flo's face is "a blank mask," for this underscores the fact that what we have just witnessed is in fact a performance. If the subject of B's eating is what prompted Flo to lick her lips, then we can read her performance as a comment on unrestrained orality. V wants to curb B's orality; Flo, on the other hand, allows B to eat freely in her kitchen and seems to advocate oral pleasure by licking her lips. By confronting V with the sight of her lips and mouth, freely moving in a kind of autoerotic gesture, Flo's act also makes explicit the link between the lips of the mouth and the lips of the genitals. By exciting V, Flo's gesture also draws her temporarily out of her repressive, rigid behavior. Flo's tongue may be read as another "secret second tongue" like J's: merely by revealing her tongue to V and B, Flo is breaking a taboo. The unsettling effect that her performance has on V reveals the power of this gesture.

What to make of these mouths that signify abundantly, but do not speak? What role do they play in B's story? Flo's mouth is disturbing and disruptive: it pulls B's story momentarily away from its only center—J; it horrifies V and mesmerizes both B and V. If there can be a center to this very decentered narrative, it might be J's mouth, which brings together B's love for J and the question of women's relation to speech. The feminine mouth is represented in dominant discourse in one of two ways: the proper, desirable feminine mouth produces no words—it is silent; the improper, undesirable feminine mouth (the fat lady's mouth) produces too many words, words that are meaningless due to their sheer abundance. In some sense, J's and B's mouths may be described in these ways. Yet these diametrically opposed representations of the feminine mouth are transformed by Hauser with her logic of both/ and, which is also the logic of her rewriting of gender. In Hauser's text, both silent and speaking feminine mouths produce meaning and both are the locus and agent of desire. In other words, the woman's mouth is always both a mysterious and desirable site of potential speech and the desiring producer of speech. This transformation of dominant representations is most apparent with J. While her characteristic silence in the novel may seem to mark her as feminine in the traditional sense, as object of discourse rather than subject/producer of it, her "secret second tongue" signifies the potential for the production of not just one language but two languages, that is, multiple meanings rather than no meaning at all. As a predominantly sexual image of the site of the production of language, the "secret second tongue" is a sign of the confluence of narrative and desire in the lesbian mouth. With these potent figures of the woman's mouth, Hauser, like Irigaray, urges woman to "open her lips" and to speak in many voices in order to discover her speech and thereby to discover her difference and her pleasure (Irigaray, *This Sex* 209). For Irigaray as for Hauser, the lips are the locus of the enigma of the feminine.[20] By turning our attention to the feminine mouth, Hauser resignifies the meaning of a forgotten and overlooked aspect of the feminine body, thus filling the blank space of the feminine with new meaning.

"A Wholesome Atmosphere of Mixed Sex": *Destabilizing the Gender Binary*

The Talking Room destabilizes the simple binary scheme for gender by rewriting gender as performative. In the world of this novel, not only is gender often at odds with sex, but subjects do not identify with only one gender or sexuality. After first creating characters whose gender and sexuality are at odds with cultural norms of masculinity and femininity, as well as of heterosexuality, Hauser then makes the doubly transgressive move of constantly shifting their gender and sexual identities. Although the gender of all of the characters violates gender norms and boundaries in one way or another, J's gender identity seems the most transgressive, which is not surprising given her alliance with the feminine conceived as radically unknowable and indefinable. J is the connection between each of the areas that Hauser explores—language, gender, the body—and she represents the possibility of crossing boundaries and transgressing rules.

Hauser's characters switch freely between butch and femme roles, masculine and feminine gender identities, homosexual and heterosexual practices, and various combinations of positions within these categories. Gender in the novel is not conceived as it is in dominant culture—as an inherent set of attributes that correspond to sex. Rather, gender is a role, an act, a performance, and sex is similarly denaturalized. Consequently, subjects can adopt any number of different gender identifications.[21] This concept of gender as imitative or performative suggests that our system of binary gender—the either/or choice of being a man or a woman—is not adequate to describe the many gender identifications that do exist and may come to exist.[22] *The Talking Room*'s characters, like Robin and Matthew in *Nightwood*, are not easily described with our existing vocabulary. For example, J's anatomical sex is female; her gender identity is both masculine and feminine; she desires both men and women; and she sleeps with both men and women. Is she a "masculine" woman? A man trapped in a woman's body, as in the nineteenth-century sexologist's notion of "the third sex"? A bisexual butch lesbian who is sometimes femme? Our severely limited vocabulary for describing gender and sexuality requires that we make such seemingly paradoxical statements as the above. The logic of binary gender and normative heterosexuality is embedded in our language, and Hauser's project is to question and rewrite these regulatory norms: she wants to expand our ability to think about gender, and creates new categories, new combinations of sex, gender, desire, and sexual practice, in order to do so.

At first glance, J and V seem to be a straightforward butch-femme couple: J is tough, surly, and masculine, while V is vulnerable, emotional, and feminine. Both J and V are self-conscious about their respective masculinity and femininity, and this self-consciousness at first seems to underscore the seemingly clear-cut division between them. But this self-consciousness points instead to the fabricated nature of these gender positions and the fact that, from scene to scene, even from moment to moment and sentence to sentence, J and V switch roles, J sometimes playing femme, V sometimes playing butch. Having already violated the dictum that gender identity mirrors anatomical sex, Hauser violates a second dictum: subjects have *one* gender identity and *one* sexuality. V is femme, yet masculine; J is butch, yet feminine. J identifies as lesbian, yet desires men as well as women. If *The Talking Room* subscribes to any logic when it comes to gender, it is the logic of "both/and," not "either/or." The ability of these characters to switch roles is one sign of the intricate interplay among sex, gender, desire, and sexual practice in the makeup of their gender identities. Although butch and femme roles are often thought to be artificial imitations of natural heterosexual behavior, this text again subverts the categories of original and copy, natural and artificial.[23] Moreover, "butch" and "femme" are only provisional terms for describing J's and V's behavior at any given moment. These terms do not by any means sum up their complex gender and sexual identities. For Hauser, gender and sexuality are the most complex of texts: they are written and they must be read. They are not natural, not rooted in the biological, and not transparent.

What makes my provisional identification of V and J as butch-femme possible? Is there a moment when these characters' personae seem to coalesce in this way? In the first scene of the novel, J and V are arguing about having had a child. J resents the fact that she is now a mother, thanks to V's coercion: "The part you forced on me—I wasn't cut out for it, don't you see? I never learned to play mother. No football coach showed me" (1). According to J, motherhood is not an inherent desire for women: it is a role to be learned and played (and it may be learned from a stereotypically masculine man), as all gender roles are in the novel. After J and V end their argument about the fact that J is now, against her will, a mother, B's narrative reverts abruptly to the past, before she was born, and recounts J's and V's past arguments about how to conceive a child. J wants to conceive a child with a man, while V prefers artificial insemination or adoption. V is very suspicious of J's sudden interest in so-called natural motherhood:

[I]t seemed perverse of J, to say the least, that she should suddenly insist she'd either have to get pregnant herself or chuck
the whole project. What was behind this sudden reversal? Aunt
V asked . . . Was her partner hoping to prove to herself that she
was after all a woman? Surely, said Aunt V with some derision,
it was a little too late in the game for *that*! (13; emphasis in original)

According to V, J's preference for getting pregnant the "natural"
way casts doubt on her butch identity as well as on her sex. When
V remarks that it is a little too late for J to "prove to herself that she
was after all a woman," it becomes clear that for V, J is not a woman.
Since it is doubtful that V questions J's status as a biological female, it is clear that V here uses "woman" to refer to a category of
gender. The language of this passage moves J back and forth across
the divide between man and woman, as well as the related, but
different, divide between butch and femme. V raises the question—
is J's gender masculine or feminine? On the one hand, since J wants
to conceive a child in the conventional way, perhaps her desire for
maternity makes her a "real woman." Similarly, her desire to conceive a child may simply be a cover for her desire to sleep with a
man, which makes her a "real woman" because she desires the
opposite sex. On the other hand, since J is butch, it is "perverse"
of her to want to conceive a child or to sleep with a man: such
desires are not congruent with her butch identification. It is also
"a little too late in the game" for these desires, because J cannot
prove herself a woman—she is not only butch, but a man (in the
sense of gender identification). But both analyses of J's gender are
unconvincing, for J is, strictly speaking, neither a woman nor a
man: technically, her biological sex is unknown to the reader, but
we can assume it is female due to the use of pronouns; she has the
gender assignment "woman"; she desires both men and women
sexually; and she identifies herself more as a man than as a woman.
The complexity of J's gender identity cannot be thought within a
binary framework, yet J is not "outside" or beyond this binary, for
she is in some way both masculine and feminine. Her gender identifications destabilize the idea of the unity and fixity of gender
identity.[24]

In order to examine Hauser's new conceptions of gender and

sexuality I will focus not on J, who may seem a more obvious choice since her gender identifications shift as easily as her desire, but on V, who speaks for a conservative view of gender, which her own behavior constantly contradicts. While J's gender and sexuality is presented as in flux from the start, Hauser traces V's complex dilemma about gender and sexuality over the course of the novel. In other words, here is a character whose gender and desire are uncontainable within traditional frameworks, yet V clings to such frameworks. V's notions about gender and her gendered behavior clash and cause conflict: this clashing is the result of conservative and new modes of gender coming head to head.

V's femininity at first seems more apparent than J's masculinity because of her self-conscious insistence upon it. V eagerly asserts her femininity because she fears that being a lesbian will diminish it, or tarnish her reputation as a "true" woman. By identifying herself as a femme, V is able to retain some sense of normal femininity while being a lesbian (which for V does not accord with womanhood) (55).[25] But her very identification with the femme role only casts doubts on her sense of her essential femininity. A femme is a lesbian who plays a feminine role, which suggests the constructed nature of gender. This differs from the notion of a feminine woman, which suggests a symmetrical and mimetic relation between sex and gender. V's protestations of her femininity only make that femininity more suspect: paradoxically, by trying to prove herself a true woman, V only proves that she is playing a role—the role of the true woman.

Although V's identification of herself as a femme indicates that she is aware to some extent of role playing and the imitative structure of gender, she clings fast to an essentialist notion of gender: she believes in a strict binary opposition between essential masculinity and essential femininity. According to V, butch women cannot want to have children through the standard means of sex with a man, because the desire for men, as well as for motherhood, is an essential feminine trait. J, being butch, is a man, according to V. V's insistence that J is in some way a man is also a denial of J's sexual interest in men. V refuses to acknowledge that J's sexuality, like her gender, is multiple and diverse; moreover, V refuses to acknowledge that this is true of herself as well. V's surprise that J may desire men is unconvincing, since she constantly refers to J's interest in sailors, stevedores, and garbage collectors throughout the novel (15, 16, 45). For V, femininity involves the most stereotypical connotations of womanhood: a true woman is fragile, emotional, domestic, weak, and passive. B gives a cynical account of V's domestic streak: "Aunt V talks about nests all the time, at home and at her office and on the radio—HOW BEST TO INVEST IN A NEST . . . Aunt V is convinced that woman was born with the nesting instinct built into her like a bed is built into those convertible sofas" (23–24). For V, there is an essential "woman" and one of her essential (or, as B puts it, "built-in") qualities is her nesting instinct. But it is V's femininity that makes her into a career woman, the one who brings home the bacon for her J-boy and her daughter B. Were it not for her "feminine" nesting instinct, V would never have become the competitive, cut-throat business(wo)man who made a killing in real estate. In her gender role, V is both an idealized 1950s mother, who advises B about how to catch a good man, and an idealized 1950s father, the stable breadwinner who provides for the family's needs. V's conservative, traditional views of sex, gender, and sexuality are also evident in her attempts to disguise her relationship with J from others by constantly referring to J as her sister or her roommate (15). V persists in seeing the relation between two women in terms of the traditional family: at one of J's departures, V cries, "[S]he was my child, my sister, put them together and they spell mother" (103). V also attempts to provide B with a "normal" family life by encouraging frequent visits from her gay male friends: "For what you need, my child, is a father image to help you grow up normal in a wholesome atmosphere of mixed sex" (27). The "sex," or more specifically, the gender, would indeed be "mixed" in the company of these men, since V has just described them as "identifying" with her as a woman more than her female friends (all lesbians) do.

Just as V takes femininity to be a set of inherent traits, so she takes her lesbianism to be the result of biological difference, and for this reason she even insists to B that she is straight. V feels that she was a "normal" woman until she had her ovaries removed. When V mentions "Jock, her second husband" and wonders "Was she wrong trading one J for another J?," B innocently yet intelligently asks, "Was he a he, was he a she?" (20). Having grown up among women who long to be husbands and men who long to be wives, B's illegitimate, sex/gender-bending question is perfectly legitimate. As B knows, a he may be a she and a she may be a he. But V assures her that this question is childish and silly: "I'm as straight as the next guy, not even bilingual, or so I have been assured by my guru. My marriage could have been successful if that woman-hating doctor hadn't removed my procreant organs. I ask you, B: why did Jock permit it, unless he too wanted to see me castrated?" (20). V's slip or pun—that she is not "bilingual" or bisexual but straight—suggests that sexuality is a kind of language or code to be learned, and yet, at other times, V seems to argue for a view of sexuality as an inherent predisposition. (In another pun, V turns "procreative" into "procreant," which rhymes with "miscreant" and alludes to the novel's suspect treatment of reproductive, familial, heterosexuality.) Although V's intention is to prove that she is straight, a normal woman, slips such as "I'm as straight as the next *guy*" make her assertion somewhat suspect and put her sex into question as much as her gender. Her claims to femininity to the contrary, V's insistence that the removal of her organs equals castration casts her as masculine. Despite V's literal equation of womanhood with ovaries, she refers to this procedure as "castration," as it is sometimes known.[26] For instance, she contends that if she hadn't had a hysterectomy as a result of a doctor's misogyny, she would have had a successful heterosexual marriage. So the presence of female reproductive organs seems to define the essence of womanhood for her: without ovaries, her marriage fails and she becomes a lesbian, which, for V, is not to be a woman.

What allows for this slide from hysterectomy to castration? Loss of the biological indicator of femininity to loss of the biological indicator of masculinity? In her marriage to Jock, just as in her relationship with J, V was the one who "br[ought] home the bacon" (21). What makes V castratable then, is the fact that she performs a masculine gender role in relation to her partners, regardless of their genders. Thinking of Jock, "Aunt V rolls her eyes. Penis envy: that was what bugged her Jock. He was much weaker, much less resourceful than she was, and so he envied her penis, and whether or not she had one had nothing whatever to do with the price of beans" (21).

Not living up to his strong, masculine name, the weak Jock envies the strong, resourceful V. Although V does not possess a penis in a literal sense, her social behavior accords with the attributes that are still identified as masculine in our culture: she is capable, resourceful, and wealthy. Although Jock may possess a penis in the literal sense, it is V who possesses a figurative penis, or phallus. Jock's envy of her is penis envy. As V puts it, "[W]hether or not she had one had nothing whatever to do with the price of beans." Given V's sense of herself and of her role in her various families, V is not a woman with a penis but a man with a vagina, in that her masculine gender role and identification seem to be joined with the anatomy of a woman. Despite her constant defense of herself as feminine, V's masculinity emerges again and again.

V's repressed masculinity is projected onto her secretary, U, who has a strange dream about having a penis, a dream with which V identifies strongly. In U's dream, as told by V, U finds herself in the men's bathroom of a subway station, wearing masculine cloth-ing (V's pants suit) and watching the men urinating. When the men, who are faceless, gradually turn to her with their flies open, "poor U had the awful suspicion or certainty that each of those faceless, identical businessmen was expecting of her that she un-zip her fly and take out her . . ." (99). At this moment in her retell-ing, V screams in imitation of U's scream upon waking. What is strange about the dream is that U is presumed to possess a penis and is expected to show it, yet the genitals of the faceless busi-nessmen are hidden, although their flies are open. What confirms their masculinity, then? How does U know that they are men? Their presence in a men's bathroom with open flies seems to confirm their masculinity (just as U is expected to open her fly, so that her sex will be revealed), whether or not they are castrated. This dream and a subsequent foray to a gay bar convinces U that she is a "male homosexual transvestite" (101), a delusion that lands her in a men-tal institution. This dream may be read as a projection of V's sense of masculinity, because U is V's double: not only are their names contiguous in the alphabet, but the letters are similar in shape; U is straight, as V feels she herself is; U is involved with an alcoholic whom she supports, as is V; U wears V's hand-me-downs; U works for V and is "a realtor's dream," just as the self-confident V feels that she is a dream of a realtor (who appropriates her secretary's dreams) (98). This story is also a favorite of V's: according to B, V has told it not just once but tells it on a regular basis (100). Of course, U is also the double of every reader, every "you" who encounters this text.

U's dream has such an effect upon U herself that the moment she wakes from it, she goes to "the nearest Queens bar for transvestites and men in leather. No ladies invited" (100). (It is worth noting that V wears leather, another manifestation of her masculinity and her identification with gay men and butch lesbians.) Hauser deftly places U, the subway station, and the transvestite bar in the borough of Queens. Hauser plays further with the pun: U will soon be "[o]utqueening every single queen in the saloon" (100), which is, of course both a "Queens bar" and a "queens' bar." U's exemplary performance has "the toughies eat[ing] out of her hand": "convinced that she was a he in drag," they soon fight over her. When the "real" queens become jealous of newcomer U's success, they take it out on her, discovering that she is a she, rather than a he. U is beaten up because of the fact that "a female . . . under the guise of a male disguised as a broad" (100) is an affront to the practice of drag, where artifice always outshines "the real thing." In drag culture, that which is artificial but appears convincingly real has much more value than that which "is" the real thing. Consequently, the real (woman) posing as a fake (man) posing as the real (woman) is an affront to the fundamental tension or opposition that structures drag performance. Esther Newton writes in *Mother Camp*, a study of drag culture, that drag is based on an opposition between the inner subjective self and the outer social self (101). For U, this is an opposition between male gender identity (inner) and female sex (outer). Drag involves a complex double inversion of these oppositions that makes it difficult to discern what is real and what is artificial: to paraphrase Newton, drag says at the same time "my appearance is feminine, but my essence is masculine" and "my appearance is masculine but my essence is feminine" (103). The reason for these seemingly contradictory statements is that drag puts into question the notion of anatomical sex as essence and, therefore, the very notion of sex. If sex does *not* determine gender identity, as drag demonstrates, then sex is not essence: if there is no inside/outside distinction, this whole series of oppositions collapses, including the opposition between essence and construct.[27]

V's masculine gender identification is also expressed in an

indirect form in her attempt to marry off J. V first proposes that J marry so that their relationship will look less suspect should anyone inquire into B's home life (44). J is cynical about the need for a "man in the house," proposing that they "get a hold of a Brooks Brothers store window dummy and sit him up in the rocking chair on the stairs, on the second landing and point him out to the social worker" (45). Though V agrees that a "dummy might do for a husband," she clings to her original idea and tries to "find a more convincing head of the household"—in other words, one more convincing than she (45). As she casts about for the right man for J's marriage of convenience, it is clear that she is trying to find a man who poses no threat to her relationship with J. This is not as easy as it sounds, since J likes men, as discussed above: "What really worried [V] was J, what J might do. If the bridegroom was a sailor, her J-boy might fall for him hook, line and sinker and leave her poor roommate the fall guy. It had happened to other married couples. No sailors. No stevedores or garbage collectors" (45). The line "It had happened to other married couples" reads in two ways, of course: "married couples" like J and V often split up because one of the partners falls for someone else (or changes their sexual orientation); and married couples, whether heterosexual or homosexual, sometimes *do* fall in love. The domesticization of desire is harshly critiqued in *The Talking Room*, whether it occurs in a heterosexual or homosexual context (since homosexuality does not provide an escape from domesticity).

J's account of V's intentions in marrying her off is very different from V's account: according to J, V has no interest in legitimizing their child but wants to create a spectacle for her own voyeuristic pleasure. J also insists that both the child and the marriage are V's attempts to keep her in line, to tie her down, as V even admits on occasion (3, 65–66). Why would V find pleasure in staging the wedding of her lover with a man? J rails at V, "Man you were itching to see me dressed up as bride for a day in 69 yards of ruffles and grandpa's longjohns under the petticoat. Man, you were wetting your drawers to watch me prance up the aisle and say I do to some cocksucking mother" (46). As J remarks, the sight of J as bride to a man (any man, it seems) would be an erotic scene for V. Is V merely the spectator of such a scene, or does she project herself onto one of the players? In a wedding, the bride, in this case J, is the center of the spectacle; she is there to be looked at, and the key spectator is, of course, the groom. Since V does not have a specific groom in mind, the place of the groom, which is also the place of the male, is an empty space for her to identify with, and, thus, to fill in. Given V's masculine identification, which emerges in her fascination with U's dream, it is safe to say that V imagines herself as the groom in this scenario. Although V's declared intention is to provide a normal family life for B by marrying J to a man and thereby making her, in some sense, a woman, V's own masculine identification would be consolidated by such an arrangement. For this reason, it is telling that this wedding never leaves the realm of V's fantasies.

V's fantasy of J's wedding is erotically charged, then, in terms of V's identification with the groom, but also in the sense that it is a fantasy about possessing the power to control J's gender identity and her desire. V wants to transform J: she doesn't want her to play the role of bride but to *be* a bride, to *be* a woman, so that V's repressed masculine identification can at last have an outlet. This is then a dream of legitimacy, but of the legitimacy of V's and J's sexuality, not of B's parentage. Always unsettled by J's shifting gender identifications and roving desire, V wants her to be fixed in *one* sex, *one* gender identity, and *one* desire; she wants her to fit into conventional narratives of gender and sexuality.[28] But V's imagined gender stability is shattered by J's biting remark about V's failure to find the right man: "[Y]ou couldn't dig up the right sucker. None wanted to be groom, each had his heart set on being the bride, each wanted to wear the veil . . ." (46). The only men that V trusts J to ignore are gay men—more specifically, queens—and, as J wryly remarks, they all want to be the bride. That these men all want to be the bride (just as V wants to be the groom) shows that no gender stabilization is possible. Their gender identities, which involve the combination of male sex, feminine gender, and desire for and sex with men, cancel out the possibility of a unified and stable gender identity and show it to be a self-legitimizing fiction.

Though most of the characters in *The Talking Room* in one way or another possess rich and multiple gender identities where masculinity and femininity proliferate rather than stagnate, one character, Uncle D, speaks for a nostalgic view of essential and distinct gender identity. One of V's closeted gay friends, Uncle D was surrounded as a child by the rhetoric of the wedding ceremony, since his parents owned a honeymoon hotel. Uncle D claims that he has always had difficulty making gender attributions, because "he eavesdropped on love before he had learned to tell a man from a woman. He still does find it difficult to tell, which, however, is not surprising, considering the present unisex trend" (49). B resembles Uncle D in her tendency to eavesdrop on love scenes: like D, she is often confused about gender, but in her case this results more from the ambiguity of her mother's and her "aunt's" gender identities than from her failure to see it with her own eyes.

Are you a man or a woman? This question plagues D and it is a question that *The Talking Room* raises in a number of ways: V asks it of J; J implicitly asks it of V; the queens ask it of U; the reader asks it of V, J, U, and all the other characters in the novel. In a situation where gender is ambiguous, which is the case in *The Talking Room*, this question is inevitable. But the novel shows that although this question is inevitable in any situation, since gender is never easily determined, it is also irrelevant, since gender is never a simple matter of either/or. It is irrelevant once one moves beyond the gender binary, which is the case in *The Talking Room*. As for Uncle D, he believes that in the good old days, this question was neither inevitable nor irrelevant, but, rather, unnecessary: "[H]e is warming himself by the gaslight of those days forever gone when a man did not have to look at a woman to know that she was a woman, when *he could tell her sex at once by the subtle music of her garments*—the rustle of the bustle, the froufrou of the frillies, the swish of the trailing train" (49; emphasis added). In Uncle D's fantasy of days gone by, sex was distinct and distinguishable, unlike the present day when even a look will not necessarily answer the question of gender.[29] But Uncle D's own language shows that these days never existed. A look or a listen was never enough because it is the garment, the cultural marker of femininity, not the woman herself, from which these "feminine" sounds issued. It is not an essential trait of woman that allowed him to "know that she was a woman" but something inessential and transferrable, that is, her garments and "their subtle music." In this way, Uncle D resembles Matthew in *Nightwood*: both characters, though surrounded by evidence of gender fluidity including themselves, cling to the fiction of distinct and stable binary gender.

That these garments could be gracing a man in drag is a possibility that Uncle D never entertains, but one that we must entertain as readers of Hauser. The "rustle," the "froufrou," and, especially, the "swish" may be produced by a man as well as a woman, by literally *any body*, no matter how that body is gendered. What Uncle D reads as a true woman may well be a man in drag, but a man in drag, doing femininity, is no less a true woman than a woman doing femininity. There is always the possibility that when we make a gender attribution, when we categorize someone as a man or a woman, we are judging a performance and not the "real thing," for there is no "real thing" when it comes to gender. This open possibility of doing gender, of performing femininity or masculinity, cancels out the idea of inherent gender identity. As Hauser shows, gender is not a question of "being" a man or a woman but of putting on an act, and this radical concept of gender as performative is one way of going beyond the limiting constraints of the gender binary.

"My Terrible Angel": J as Intermediary

In an odd way, J is connected more directly with writing in the novel than B, although J writes very little and B is, after all, the teller of the tale. When V gives J a blank book in which to write as a way to fill up her time, J writes only two things. B later finds in the book a picture of a cross and a line copied from Rainer Maria Rilke—"JEDER ENGEL IST SCHRECKLICH"—"Every angel is terrifying."[30] J may seem to confirm her emptiness by writing next to nothing, but what little she does write is also a cryptic and enigmatic text that resounds with meaning. B and V both read this text of J's, trying to derive a clue, some meaning, from it (just as they are compulsive readers of J herself). V fixates on the first letter of the first word—J—reducing the already scanty text to a mere referent to her lover's identity: "Aunt V will open the book and stare at the single line and speak the first letter. J" (68). In her search for a referent, V's literal approach to language is again revealed. B, however, focuses on the blankness of the book and the cross, believing herself to be the only reader/interpreter to have done so: "Every angel . . . There's nothing else inside that book, not another line or word. The pages are empty. But on the page next to the last, in the left corner, I've noticed a small cross in ink. I doubt that anyone outside of me has noticed it. Mom's unwritten poems" (68). J's blankness and her book's near blankness make them spaces of potential writing, just as the O's blankness, noted elsewhere by B, may be read instead as the O's fullness. For B, J and her book are not blank, but are "unwritten": they are texts that exist in a strange state of being that is marked by negation (*un*written) but is also marked by potential (they will or could be written). In some ways, we might read B's narrative, *The Talking Room*, as the fulfillment of this potential: she completes J's "unwritten poems"; she fills in the blank of her mother's identity by making her a character in her narrative.[31] She gives form and shape to J in an inversion of the mother/daughter relationship. J's neglect of her amounts to an unwritten account of their relationship; B takes this emptiness and makes it signify, endows it with meaning. Just as B fills up the emptiness of her mouth or stomach, so she instinctively fills up the emptiness of the blank page.

The meaning of the line that J copies from Rilke is significant as well. What does it mean that J's one piece of writing is a line about angels? In copying the line from Rilke, J may seem to be performing her muteness by citing the words of a male poet, rather than writing her "own" words.[32] The cross may also seem to indicate J's belief in male authority, but this too is undercut by the reference to the angel, who threatens all hierarchies. J herself is referred to as an angel throughout the novel. V calls J "my terrible angel" (56); B also thinks of J as an angel, likening her to one upon her return: J "returns from the unknown" as an angel would (144).[33] So, in copying Rilke's line, J is writing about herself. For J, as for Rilke, the angel is terrifying, but why?[34] In its relation to the unknown, or, as B says elsewhere, the "otherworldly," the angel inspires fear (155). Irigaray has written extensively of the terrifying angel in her work on a new ethical relation between the sexes.[35] For Irigaray, angels are boundary crossers, like Hauser's characters as well as those of Woolf, Barnes, and Winterson. Both divine and human, male and female (and yet neither), angels are androgynous, other-sexed beings that function as intermediaries between God and man, heaven and earth, man and woman.

The angel would be a key means of enabling a revision of relations between the sexes according to Irigaray, and, as such, it is a privileged figure. It is the angel's relationship to sexuality, the sexual act itself, that would help to establish this new relation between the sexes. Irigaray writes that the angel is "a representation of a sexuality that has never been incarnated" (*An Ethics*, "Sexual Difference" 16).[36] J bears a similar relationship to sexuality. Certainly, V's references to J as a terrible angel always have the proprietary ring of lover's words. Herein lies some of J's mystery—her status as enigma: she points to an unrealized future.

The angel confounds not just sexual distinctions but physical distinctions as well. This quality is connected to the angel's traditional status as messenger between heaven and earth, between different worlds. B and V must constantly deal with J's frequent and prolonged absences and with her abrupt returns into their lives. In her movement between different worlds, J, like the angel, does not abide by the same rules of physical existence as mortals. "The angel is that which unceasingly *passes through the envelopes(s)* or *container(s)*, goes from one side to the other" (*An Ethics* 15; emphasis in original). In passing from world to world, J functions as a messenger. Although silent, her few words are laden with meaning, as we saw with her "book of unwritten poems." Irigaray takes the traditional association of angels with messengers and exploits it for its subversive potential: "[The angel] is sent or comes, from heaven, on a mission, to do a job. In fact the angel always returns to heaven, goes home, to the other side of the ultimate veil . . . From beyond the angel returns with inaudible or unheard of words in the here and now. Like an inscription written in invisible ink on a fragment of body, skin, membrane, veil, colorless and unreadable until it interacts with the right substance, the matching body" (*Sexes and Genealogies* 36–37).[37] The final pages of *The Talking Room* involve one of J's many returns from the unknown. B alludes to her mysterious absence and return in terms similar to those of Irigaray's passage. J's return is accompanied by rain, which underscores her immateriality and her connection to the fluid rather than the solid.[38] She brings with her traces of the other world from which she comes:

> Hi, kid, mom whispered as she crept into my room out of the rain . . . Her rain-glazed face was swimming out of the door frame, toward my bed. And there was on her breath that mysterious odor I well remember from other nights when she'd surface after her trip through oblivion: an odor no longer of gin but of something highly distilled, rarefied and almost otherworldly like a liquid reserved for angels. (154–55)

J returns to this world from another world, one like Woolf's where "other sexes loo[k] through the branches of other trees at other skies" (*A Room* 88). And she bears a message from this other world, much like the angel does from the ideal world of Irigaray's imagining where an ethical relation between the sexes would be possible. What is this message? That in order for true difference to be realized, there must be a meeting, a reconnection, of masculine and feminine, which may take the form of a confounding of opposition. J is a living example of such an "other sex," existing on the border between masculine and feminine. Like Bernard in the last pages of *The Waves* or *Nightwood*'s figures of the third sex, the doll, and the prince, the angel is a potent figure of these other sexes from other worlds. It stands between, on the border, confounding rather than invoking opposition. These figures of other sexes represent the possibility of a state in which our limited and limiting categories for gender identity simply do not apply, and with them, all other markers of difference and hierarchy are obliterated.

FIVE

A FEMINIST ETHICS OF LOVE
Jeanne Winterson's
Written on the Body

> I will explore you and mine you and you will redraw me
> according to your will. We shall cross one another's bound-
> aries and make ourselves one nation.
> —Jeanette Winterson, *Written on the Body*

> How can I say "you," when you are always other? How
> can I speak to you? You remain in flux, never congealing
> or solidifying. What will make that current flow into
> words? . . . These streams are without fixed banks, this body
> without fixed boundaries.
> —Luce Irigaray, *This Sex Which Is Not One*

Like *The Waves, Written on the Body* is a self-reflexive text preoccupied with language; like *Nightwood*, it confounds simple gender
categorization; and like *The Talking Room*, it is a meditation on love
and loss. As the narrator struggles with the loss of her beloved to
cancer, she attempts to literally recreate her through and as a written text.[1] Writing becomes a manifestation of passionate sexual
love that enables the lover to cross the boundary between self and
other and thereby fully inhabit the other's being. The central trope
of the novel—writing as bodily act, the body as written text—is
another trope of the liminal, similar to Woolf's "little language,"
Barnes's third sex, and Hauser's ambiguously gendered characters. For Winterson, to touch the flesh and to love the body is also
to write upon it and to read it. Through these metaphors, the flesh,
typically considered the marker of the boundary between self and
other, becomes the gateway to immersion in the other's being. Due
to the central character's nearly insatiable desire for this immersion, the possibility of violating this boundary looms large in the

novel. Just as Winterson explores the space between self and other, word and object, so she explores the space between masculine and feminine. While Barnes and Hauser depict characters who may be described as both masculine and feminine in terms of their behavior and desire, Winterson goes about creating gender ambiguity very differently. She depicts a nearly featureless narrator (we are only told of its romantic history) and gives us no clear signals as to its gender such as gendered pronouns or a name. Despite this refusal to mark gender, at the same time the novel offers many hints that "it" is in fact a she. By leaving her narrator's gender a question, yet loading the text with suggestions that "it" is in fact a woman, Winterson boldly claims universality for a feminine and lesbian subject position, an idea advanced in Monique Wittig's theoretical writing.

Written on the Body explores the intersubjective, ethical ramifications of the meeting of opposed terms that are the focus of this study. By dwelling on the contact between one and another in a loving, passionate relationship, the novel traces a complex tension between respect for the other and the violation of the other. In this focus on the ethics of love, the novel details a poetics of fleshly, mundane, earthly love; it dwells on the caress, the embrace, and the touch. Yet it also suggests that such love has a spiritual dimension, one that transcends the everyday and earthly. This meeting of mundane and spiritual, like the meeting of masculine and feminine within the subject in Barnes, Woolf, and Hauser, echoes Luce Irigaray's theory of the sensible transcendental. All are a means of restoring the repudiated feminine, in all its various associations, to its central place in Western thought.

"I Want to Do the Right Thing": The Ethics of Love

More than the other novels studied here, *Written on the Body* raises the question of the ethical ramifications of these meetings and crossings of opposed terms, because the meeting in this text is an intersubjective one. What does it mean to attempt to become one with the other? Although the narrator wishes to consume her lover, Louise, early in their relationship, by the end of the novel the narrator begins to see love in different terms, terms that allow her to be joined with Louise, yet not be consumed by nor consume her. The narrator discovers that "true love" requires an ethical relationship to the other. My reading of *Written on the Body*'s ethics of love is based on Irigaray's concept of the sensible transcendental, as discussed in chapter 1. The two manifestations of this concept that bear directly on the novel are the immediate and the passion called wonder.

A central aspect of Irigaray's theory of the ethics of sexual difference is her inquiry into that which has been excluded from metaphysics—the immediate or the sensible—because it has been relegated to the feminine. Although the exclusion of the immediate is a critical problem, it is frequently overlooked: "Few people worry about finding new ways to experience passion, or passions, about working out a new pathos, or rather a more ethical spirit, rooted in the world of the senses. . . . the problem of the relation to the immediate has not been resolved" (*Sexes and Genealogies* 115). In order for "our relation to the immediate" to be "resolved," we must first of all begin to admit that there is such a thing as the immediate, and we must acknowledge that the immediate has been problematized due to its connection with the feminine, the body, and the material. The issue of the immediate is directly related to the simultaneous insistence upon difference and lack of genuine sexual difference. In a pivotal passage, Irigaray asks why a genuine sexual difference "has not had its chance to develop, either empirically or transcendentally" (*An Ethics* 15). One aspect of the lack of genuine sexual difference is the split between the sensible and transcendental, which would be resolved by the meeting of these realms in the sensible transcendental. In answer to her own question, she alludes to her key notion of the sensible transcendental without naming it as such:[2]

It is surely a question of the dissociation of body and soul, of sexuality and spirituality, of the lack of a passage for the spirit, for the god, between the inside and the outside, the outside and the inside, and of their distribution between the sexes in the sexual act. Everything is constructed in such a way that these realities remain separate, even opposed to one another. So that they neither mix, marry, nor form an alliance. Their wedding is always being put off to a beyond, a future life, or else devalued,

> felt and thought to be less worthy in comparison to the marriage
> between the mind and God in a transcendental realm where all
> ties to the world of sensation have been severed. (*An Ethics* 15)

Irigaray envisions a restoration of and to the senses—a healing of
the breach between the sensible and the transcendental. Irigaray's
language is sweeping in this passage because the nature of this
breach is immense. Margaret Whitford writes that through the
concept of the sensible transcendental, "Irigaray is positing that
the oppositions might come into relation—the mother and father,
the Sensible and the Intelligible, the immediate and the transcen-
dent, the material and the ideal—in imaginary and symbolic
processes, that is, that each sex might be able to assume its own divisions" (*Luce Irigaray* 122). For Irigaray, the oppositions come into
relation in the meeting of man and woman. However, to take her
point to its conclusion, if "each sex" is to truly "assume its own
divisions," then each sex would bear the fruit of this encounter
and would be the meeting place of masculine and feminine, or the
realization of genuine sexual difference. The sexed subject conceived in this way should be understood as "other-sexed," and
only possible in the context of a genuine sexual difference.

The ethical encounter that Irigaray alludes to involves not the
merging of self and other but the meeting of self and other. The
male-female couple is her focus because of their inherent difference: "[T]hey are irreducible one to the other" (*An Ethics* 12). When
such an encounter truly takes place (and her language makes clear
that she believes it has not), the boundaries between the lovers
remain fully intact despite the intense "joining" that takes place
between them. Irigaray writes: "Who or what the other is, I never
know. But the other who is forever unknowable to me is the one
who differs from me sexually. This feeling of surprise, astonish-
ment and wonder in the face of the unknowable ought to be returned
to its locus: that of sexual difference" (*An Ethics* 13). Many negative emotions factor into the relation between man and woman,
"but not that wonder which beholds what it sees always as if for
the first time, never taking hold of the other as its object. It does
not try to seize, possess, or reduce this object, but leaves it subjective, still free" (*An Ethics* 13).[3] The relationship between Winterson's
narrator and Louise reaches this point in their last encounter in

the novel. Wonder possesses a healing power, because it takes place at the junction of the sensible and the transcendental. Irigaray writes that wonder is a

> birth into a transcendence, that of the other, still in the world of the senses ("sensible"), still physical and carnal, and already spiritual. Is it the place of incidence and junction of body and spirit, which has been covered over again and again, hardened through repetitions that hamper growth and flourishing? . . . Wonder would be the passion of the encounter between the most material and the most metaphysical, of their possible conception and fecundation one by the other. A third dimension. An intermediary. Neither the one nor the other. Which is not to say neutral or neuter. The forgotten ground of our condition . . . (*An Ethics* 82)

Irigaray bases the possibility of a genuine sexual difference in an irreducible otherness that man and woman find in each other.[4] This wonder is not the exclusive property of the sexually differentiated, however. To argue that, as Irigaray does, is to reduce the complexity of sexual or gender difference within the subject as well as between subjects who are presumably identical as men or women. If we think of Irigaray's writings on ethics in dialogue with her 1970s writings on women such as "When Our Lips Speak Together" (*This Sex*), it is possible to bridge this seeming gap. The encounter between man and woman, as Irigaray herself acknowledges, is fraught with negativity because of the history of the relation between the sexes. That is, the very division that the sensible transcendental seeks to overcome is liable to threaten this encounter. As Irigaray writes, "[B]etween man and woman . . . [come] attraction, greed, possession . . ." (13). The encounter between subjects of the "same sex" is less likely to be fraught with such issues because a history of domination between them does not exist, while it certainly does between men and women. This history of the male subordination of women is present in every encounter between the sexes. For Irigaray to insist on wonder in the heterosexual encounter and to largely dismiss the possibility of these passions occurring in the homosexual encounter is to risk simplifying homosexuality by equating it with narcissism. That is, she is blind to the difference within women as well as between women (and between men), despite her constant insistence upon the recognition of difference.

"We shall cross one another's boundaries":
Drawing the Line between Self and Other

The mutual exchange and reciprocity discussed in the passage from *Written on the Body* used as an epigraph to this chapter represent the ideal that is only occasionally grasped by the narrator in her desire to be one with Louise. The fact that the narrator desires such a close connection to her lover is important in and of itself. The early parts of the novel involve two simultaneous narratives: the ongoing narrative about the relationship with Louise and the episodic narrative of her many affairs prior to Louise. Most of these affairs are with married women and most last under six months, due to the narrator's circadian clock, as she puts it.[5] The stories of these affairs provide a necessary counterpoint to the story of Louise, for the narrator undergoes a profound reeducation about love by means of this relationship. She realizes that while she has had many affairs due to her disdain for serious relationships, especially marriage, and her belief that they are passionless, a kind of love is possible in which she may have both passion and commitment (79). She finds just this with Louise. Her jaded view of love, as represented by her previous, more lighthearted affairs, nearly compromises her relationship with Louise, despite its basis in love. When they first become lovers, the narrator is quick to declare her love, but Louise cautions her to be careful to mean what she says (53). Louise is extremely wary of the narrator due to her past exploits.

Throughout this narrative, the narrator traces her development from heartless Lothario to committed, responsible, and deeply passionate lover. The narrator is rather self-conscious about the issue of ethics in love. At one point, she questions her own ethical failings as well as those of most people (43). Louise stands in the position of "saviour": through loving her fully, the narrator will be able to escape her past (77). But the narrator must first fail Louise before she learns to love her as she is meant to be loved. In fact, the impetus for the novel is the narrator's desire to understand "where I went wrong" (17). Throughout the novel, the narrator's understanding of love expands and matures: she comes to learn that intimacy is "the recognition of another person that is deeper than consciousness, lodged in the body more than held in the mind" (82). Yet despite this realization early in her relationship with Louise, it takes her some time to act on this knowledge. She also revises this definition somewhat, eventually "recognizing" Louise on levels other than the physical. When she leaves Louise upon learning that she has cancer, she does so because Louise's husband Elgin, an oncologist, will continue to care for her only on this condition. Despite the concern for Louise's health upon which this decision is based, the narrator makes the mistake of not recognizing Louise's wish to stay with her. Instead, the narrator only recognizes her own sense of what is right, and by completely overlooking Louise's sense of what is right, she betrays her. After their separation, the narrator begins to think of Louise differently, and this indicates the distance she has come in her awareness of what love can be in the fullest sense. While praying for Louise, the narrator begins "[t]o think of Louise in her own right, not as my lover, not as my grief. It helped me to forget myself and that was a great blessing" (153). At the same time, because she is thinking of Louise in her own right, the narrator begins to doubt her decision to leave Louise to Elgin: "'You made a mistake,' said the voice" (153). Part of this process of understanding love anew involves the narrator's gradual realization of the way in which she has failed Louise by leaving her. In the act of writing this narrative, she recognizes that to leave Louise was to fail her. After several moments when she doubts her actions (148, 153), the narrator finally admits that "I had failed Louise and it was too late. What right had I to decide how she should live? What right had I to decide how she should die?" (156–57). After her employer and one-time lover Gail Right confirms the narrator's own opinion (and Gail Right's name tells us how to regard her views), the narrator decides to return to London to look for Louise (158–59). Although she does not find her, she leaves a letter with her address, which leads to their eventual reunion on the last page of the novel.

The narrator's love for Louise is so profound that she wants to immerse herself fully in Louise's being, primarily her physical being. As Winterson writes, "I didn't only want Louise's flesh, I wanted her bones, her blood, her tissues, the sinews that bound her together. I would have held her to me though time had stripped away the tones and textures of her skin" (51). This passage is notable for its hyperbole. The narrator has always guarded herself against full attachment and commitment, yet now she wants these as well as complete absorption in every aspect of her lover's being. Because her desire for Louise is so extensive that it is boundless, she speaks constantly of crossing all boundaries between them. Yet there is a kind of violence implicit here in her desire to have Louise as a collection of body parts ("her bones, her blood, her tissues"). This violence comes full circle in the central section of the text, entitled "THE CELLS, TISSUES, SYSTEMS AND CAVITIES OF THE BODY," in which the narrator literally seeks to become one with each part of Louise's body, using the language of medical textbooks to get under Louise's skin. In what follows, I refer to this section as the body parts section.

The narrator's desire for full connection is not always so excessive, however. It is tempered, for example, in a passage where she discusses the "tie" between them. Although she and Louise are "held by a single loop of love," it is a straight loop with "no sharp twists or sinister turns" (88). She compares this "loop of love" to the actual rope that was used to tie two fighters in Renaissance Italy. This is not her wish; instead, she wants a clean, straight line between them: "I want the hoop around our hearts to be a guide not a terror" (88). At this point in the text, Winterson uses writing and reading as metaphors for the connection between the narrator and her lover, and these best convey the nature of this tie.

> Articulacy of the fingers . . . signing on the body body longing. Who taught you to write in blood on my back? Who taught you to use your hands as branding irons? You have scored your name into my shoulders, referenced me with your mark . . .
>
> Written on the body is a secret code only visible in certain lights; the accumulations of a lifetime gather there . . . I like to keep my body rolled up away from prying eyes. Never unfold too much, tell the whole story. I didn't know that Louise would have reading hands. She has translated me into her own book. (89)

In this passage the narrator and Louise switch roles: it is usually the narrator who is the lover and Louise who is the beloved. The lover here does a certain violence to the beloved's body, branding and scoring marks upon her flesh. But these are marks upon the surface of the body and they merely add to "the accumulations of a lifetime"—the scars and marks of daily living and aging. The act of reading that is described in the rest of the passage is a loving act: having sheltered herself and her story, the narrator now opens herself like a book under Louise's hands. These hands have a double function, which is both to write upon her body and to read her body. The "translation" described in the last line of the passage is a transfer into another medium, which does not irrevocably alter the narrator or her story.[6] It is not a violent appropriation or violation like the narrator's forced entry into Louise's body in the body parts section. Writing and reading metaphors serve to balance the narrator's desire for immersion with ethical respect for the other. Such metaphors imply that there is always a remainder: she cannot fully have Louise, but only a version or interpretation of her, just as Louise cannot fully have her.

At these moments when the narrator balances desire for immersion in the other and recognition of the other in her otherness, there are striking parallels between Winterson's novel and Irigaray's classic text on the union between women lovers, "When Our Lips Speak Together," the source of the second epigraph to this chapter. What unites the speaker and her lover in Irigaray's text is first their similarity, from which everything else springs. She writes: "We live by twos . . . Our resemblance does without semblances: for in our bodies we are already the same. Touch yourself, touch me, you'll 'see'" (*This Sex* 216). Their giving is reciprocal, since to love the other is to love the self: "When you say I love you . . . you're saying I love myself . . . That 'I love you' is neither gift nor debt" (206). As in *Written on the Body*, the issue of language is central to the issue of connection and boundary crossing: Irigaray writes of "find[ing] our body's language" (214). Such a bodily language will facilitate the fluidity of the boundaries between the two women: "Let's hurry and invent our own phrases. So that everywhere and always we can continue to embrace . . . We shall pass imperceptibly through every barrier, unharmed, to find each other" (215).

Irigaray writes of a kind of alternative space or relation that is possible between women, in comparison to the place in which women find themselves in Western culture—a subordinate place in the patriarchal, heterosexual economy that divides women from each other. Similarly, in *Written on the Body*, it is the narrator's investment in a limited notion of love drawn from the heterosexual economy that divides her from Louise. Irigaray writes: "We put ourselves into watertight compartments, break ourselves up into parts, cut ourselves in two, and more. Whereas we are always one and the other, at the same time. If we separate ourselves that way, we 'all' stop being born" (217). Women are deprived of life itself in this economy because of the insistence on clear boundaries between all beings. Women must escape in order to survive. Irigaray describes the deadening effect of being immersed in the patriarchal economy in this way:

> How can we speak so as to escape from their compartments, their schemas, their distinctions and oppositions . . . How can we shake off the chain of these terms, free ourselves from their categories . . . *You know that we are never completed, but that we only embrace ourselves whole. That one after another, parts—of the body, of space, of time—interrupt the flow of our blood.* Paralyze, petrify, immobilize us. Make us paler. Almost frigid. (212; emphasis added)

This is precisely what we see in the body parts section of the novel, in reverse. Having lived fully in, through, and with Louise, the narrator is stunned by loss when she leaves Louise to Elgin. She then attempts to recreate Louise but uses the language of Western medicine to do so. The more she thinks of Louise in this light, the less alive she becomes. Over the course of this section, this same categorization and negation that Irigaray details take place. Rather than bring Louise to life, as is the narrator's wish, she renders her lifeless, piece by piece.[7]

The narrator violates Louise, from a metaphorical standpoint, when she takes the notion of crossing boundaries too far during their separation by using a Western medical approach to the body. That she rewrites Louise's body in this context at the same time that she literally abandons Louise to Western medical care makes this violent rewriting all the more violent. When Louise asked the narrator early in their relationship if she would stay with her unconditionally, clearly she was referring to the narrator's inevitable discovery of her illness. Just as she fails Louise by leaving her, so she fails her by attempting to invade her body much as the cancer itself has done. The particular way in which she approaches Louise's body—as a collection of discrete parts—also constitutes a failure. Ironically, such an approach overlooks the specific way that cancer attacks the body. The narrator makes several references to the anomaly that cancer is when considered from the standpoint of Western medicine, yet she herself does not follow this lead. Cancer is holistic in its invasion of the body, while Western medicine isolates the body into discrete parts (105, 175). She explains metastasis in this way: "Cancer has a unique property; it can travel from the site of origin to distant tissues . . . In doctor-think the body is a series of bits to be isolated and treated as necessary, that the body in its very disease may act as a whole is an upsetting concept. Holistic medicine is for faith healers and crackpots, isn't it?" (175). The narrator fails to understand that she herself uses "doctor-think" to recreate and know Louise more fully when she leaves her. She seeks to be one with her, paradoxically, by dividing her up and knowing each part of her, an approach that is anything but holistic. Louise's style of loving should also have given her a hint: "It was necessary to engage her whole person. Her mind, her heart, her soul and her body could only be present as two sets of twins. She would not be divided from herself" (68). The narrator has previously approached relationships in just the opposite way: relationships engaged her body and her passion, but never any other part of her. To some extent, this is also true of her relationship with Louise. The narrator is attentive to the body in and of itself and to the bodily nature of their love, at the expense of other aspects of their connection. Only after leaving Louise and trying to find her again is she able to see that she has made an error and must bring back into their love those other parts of herself, primarily her faith and her trust.

Although the body parts section begins with an attempt to become more intimate with Louise, in the narrator's sense of "recognition," it takes several turns away from this initial aim.

> If I could not put Louise out of my mind I would drown myself
> in her. Within the clinical language . . . I found a love-poem to
> Louise. I would go on knowing her, more intimately than the
> skin, hair and voice that I craved. I would have her plasma, her
> spleen, her synovial fluid. I would recognise her even when her
> body had long since fallen away. (111)

The effect of this method of knowing her is to depersonalize her
utterly. By studying an anatomy textbook, she does not learn about
Louise's skin and organs; instead, she learns about generic skin
and organs. The body represented in the anatomy textbook is not
Louise's body, but any body (and at the same time, no body).[8]
Simply reading about biology and anatomy is not going to bring
Louise to her on this level. It is even arguable whether this is the
level at which the spirit of a human being exists. It seems that the
narrator has taken her former style of loving, which stopped at
the physical and passionate, and has pushed that to an extreme,
hoping that this will be the equivalent of "true love." This may be
due to her new definition of intimacy as "the recognition of another
person that is deeper than consciousness, *lodged in the body* more
than held in the mind" (82; emphasis added). Privileging the body
over the mind is as great a mistake as privileging the mind over
the body. A true recognition of the other would be an ethical
encounter, which would involve a meeting of mind and body, just
as it is a meeting of self and other. Although the narrator believes
that she can avoid death and mortality through this approach to
Louise, she in a sense kills the real Louise and replaces her with
Louise as dissected corpse, the material basis of the anatomy lessons she teaches herself. The language of death even creeps in to
these sections more and more.[9]

In the section on the cavities of the body, the narrator very
explicitly uses such a language: "Let me penetrate you. I am the
archaeologist of tombs. I would devote my life to marking your
passageways, the entrances and exits of that impressive mauso-
leum, your body" (119). Of course, since the narrator is contem-
plating her beloved's eventual death, she is bound to see Louise's
body as her grave. Yet it seems that she metaphorically assists in
the process by so relishing her role as mortician, as in her reference to "embalm[ing] you in my memory" (119). Because losing

Louise has made her feel dead, the narrator wants to kill her in turn: "You must be rid of life as I am rid of life" (119). Such remarks make it clear that the narrator is conscious of and deliberate about the language that she is using. The reason for this attempt to metaphorically invade Louise's body is at last made clear. The narrator writes of "knowing" Louise externally by appreciating her physical beauty, but she sees a vast gap between knowing the surface and knowing the depth: "I have held your head in my hands but I have never held you. Not you in your spaces, spirit, electrons of life" (120). The narrator's desire to penetrate Louise actually preceded their separation. "Mining" is a common metaphor in the text for the narrator's lovemaking, whether or not it is with Louise. She speaks of "explor[ing] you and min[ing] you" (20), as well as of her queasiness about "plumbing" the depths of her lovers (17). She often uses the term "pushing into" as well (110, 137). Related to this series of metaphors are analogies between a woman's sex and a shell (15, 73), and the narrator occasionally brags about her violent penetration of these shells. She notes, "I've . . .blown into the hollows of many [shells]. Where I've left cracking too severe to mend the owners have simply turned the bad part to the shade" (15). Coupled with the violent metaphors of the body parts section, the overall picture is one of the violation of the other.

The ethical dimension of love that the narrator eventually discovers has a spiritual dimension as well, which is suggested through the narrator's many references to the pilgrim. The first reference is to a print in Louise's house, of Edward Burne-Jones's *Love and the Pilgrim*. This comes into play early in their affair when the narrator is quick to say "I love you," and Louise cautions her to "Never say you love me until that day when you have proved it" (54). The narrator then reflects on *Love and the Pilgrim*, which hangs in the room where they have just made love: "An angel in clean garments leads by the hand a traveller footsore and weary. The traveller is in black and her cloak is still caught by the dense thicket of thorns from which they have both emerged. Would Louise lead me so? Did I want to be led?" (54) . The narrator is correct in her judgment that "As a lover I was lethal" (53). Not fully present, because she is still wrapping up her relationship with Jacqueline, the narrator is far from ready to be led by Louise.

First, she must wander through that "dense thicket" alone—her self-exile from Louise.[10]

The narrator muses again on the image of the pilgrim, after comparing being held by Louise to being rocked in a boat. She imagines medieval pilgrims setting sail, secure in their faith and belief in God. In this image, Louise is the boat, the narrator the pilgrim: "Louise let me sail in you over these spirited waves. I have the hope of a saint in a coracle . . . Love it was that drove them forth. Love that brought them home again" (81). The narrator feels herself capable of trusting Louise and following her faithfully, but this is prior to learning that Louise has cancer. She thinks she is ready to give up her past and become someone new with Louise: "Louise, I would gladly fire the past for you, go and not look back . . . I know what it will mean to redeem myself from the accumulations of a lifetime" (81). As the story plays out, however, she discovers that she is far from ready. The narrator tellingly transforms the pilgrim's voyage into a bodily voyage as they begin making love again: "Eyes closed I began a voyage down her spine, the cobbled road of hers that brought me to a cleft and a damp valley" (82). Compared to the open-ended, dangerous voyage of emotional intimacy, the voyage of physical intimacy is easy and pleasant. She seems to realize this herself towards the end of the novel, after she has returned to London to seek out Louise. She questions every move that she has made, particularly her failure to accept Louise's refusal to go back to Elgin. In this context, she refers to Louise again as her guide and potential saviour. "Louise, stars in your eyes, my own constellation. I was following you faithfully but I looked down. You took me out beyond the house, over the roofs, way past commonsense and good behaviour. No compromise. I should have trusted you but I lost my nerve" (187). By initiating their reconciliation, the narrator finally puts her faith in Louise, becoming pilgrim to her angel/saviour as in *Love and the Pilgrim*.[11]

The love between the narrator and Louise, particularly when they are reunited at the end of the novel, involves wonder in the Irigarayan sense because it involves the unification of body and soul, the sexual and the spiritual. While several critics see this union as "fantastic," I would argue that it is important that we see it as real and realizable.[12] The narrator's shock and surprise when she opens her door and sees Louise indicate wonder, not the fantastic, imaginary nature of Louise's return. Upon seeing Louise, the narrator needs to touch her to be convinced that she's real: "I put out my hand and felt her fingers, she took my fingers and put them to her mouth . . . Am I stark mad? She's warm" (190). The expansiveness of her vision as she describes the scene of their reunion is now the measure (to use the narrator's own metaphor) of love, rather than loss being the measure of love, as was the case at the beginning of the novel (9). "The windows have turned into telescopes. Moon and stars are magnified in this room. The sun hangs over the mantelpiece. I stretch out my hand and reach the corners of the world. The world is bundled up in this room" (190).[13] Here Winterson uses the same language to describe the reunion that she used to describe the room in which Louise and the narrator first made love: "The walls . . . were breathing. I could feel them moving under my touch . . . The light, channeled by the thin air, heated the panes of glass too hot to open. We were magnified in this high wild room. You and I could reach the ceiling and the floor and every side of our loving cell" (51). This earlier scene is just as fantastic as the final reunion scene, but there is not doubt that it takes place: their love is so profound and so transformative that it alters material objects. Such a meeting on all levels, such a crossing of strict boundaries, is possible. Winterson achieves the crossing of boundaries in another context through the genderless narrative voice.

"Male or Female": The Genderless Narrative Voice

I thought you were the most beautiful creature male or female I had ever seen. (Winterson, *Written on the Body* 84)

While Winterson's narrator is technically ungendered, there are many wry hints that "it" is in fact a "she." For example, we learn of the narrator's revolutionary acts with her radical feminist girlfriend Inge, and it is impossible to imagine Inge as anything but a lesbian (22–23). We also learn of the narrator's dream about a girlfriend who sets a mousetrap for her mailman's penis because she is annoyed with him. She tells the narrator that she has nothing to worry about; that is to say, her genitals could not be caught in such a trap (41–42).[14] On a more serious note, many of the narrator's girlfriends refer to her lovemaking abilities and the implication seems to be that she knows and loves them in a way that their husbands and boyfriends cannot. The narrator's refusal to equate love with reproduction suggests that her brand of loving is nonreproductive, that is, lesbian (108). There are also extratextual reasons for reading the narrator's gender as female; Winterson discusses her lesbianism as well as the autobiographical nature of all of her texts (particularly *Oranges Are Not the Only Fruit* and *Written on the Body*) in interviews.[15]

In addition to the many plot "hints" that the narrator is a woman, many passages establish the strong similarities between the lovers. Here, again, Winterson is rather direct. In the following passage, the narrator comments on the differences between heterosexual and lesbian love precisely in terms of the question of difference.

> I thought difference was rated to be the largest part of sexual attraction but there are so many things about us that are the same.
> Bone of my bone. Flesh of my flesh. To remember you it's my own body I touch. Thus she was, here and here. (129–30)

One of the means by which the heterosexual economy operates is of course this idea that "opposites attract." By contrast, the narrator discovers through Louise the intense allure of sameness. The narrator also states, while separated from Louise: "You are still the colour of my blood. You are my blood. When I look in the mirror it's not my own face I see. Your body is twice. Once you once me. Can I be sure which is which?" (99). These passages, in their freshness and beauty, resemble Irigaray's "When Our Lips Speak Together." Despite this, the narrator occasionally slips into a dangerous kind of boundary crossing, as in the body parts section as well as in other passages such as this: "She was my twin and I lost her. Skin is waterproof but my skin was not waterproof against Louise. She flooded me and she has not drained away. I am still wading through her, she beats upon my doors and threatens my innermost safety" (163).[16] There is a certain danger even in these positive evocations of connection through similarity; it is due to the all-consuming nature of their love, which threatens the loss of self.

Why does Winterson leave gender unmarked in the standard sense by eliminating gendered pronouns, yet load the text with other marks of gender, as discussed above?[17] It is doubtful that Winterson finds concealment in and of itself subversive. Rather, what is subversive occurs on the level of language. The use of the pronoun "she" immediately locates women in a subordinate position in the social order. According to Monique Wittig, to refuse to gender women in this way grants them a different status, the status of the universal, a position historically available only to men.[18]

Wittig is concerned with gender not just as a social category but as a linguistic category, and she notes how these two categories inform each other.[19] For Wittig, the foundation of oppression is difference—the male/female as well as the heterosexual/homosexual oppositions.[20] For that reason, she takes a position quite different from Irigaray's regarding difference. For Wittig, difference must be abolished, not rediscovered, for difference is synonymous with "domination." On this point, she writes that "[t]he concept of difference has nothing ontological about it. It is only the way that the masters interpret a historical situation of domination. The function of difference is to mask at every level the conflicts of interest, including ideological ones" (29). Difference and gender mark women only, not men, for "the masculine is not the masculine but the general" (60). Wittig's position on gender is the opposite of Irigaray's. Instead of the masculine being the only sex, the feminine is the only sex in Wittig's account: "[T]he category of sex is the category that sticks to women, for only they cannot be conceived outside of it. Only *they* are sex" (8; emphasis in original). For this reason, in order to assume a universal position, a woman must be de-gendered as Winterson's narrator is. Language provides this possibility of freeing women of their entrapment in the particular: "Gender then must be destroyed. The possibility of its destruction is given through the very exercise of language. For each time I say 'I,' I reorganize the world from my point of view and through abstraction I lay claim to universality. This fact holds true for every locutor" (81). In Wittig's terms, the fact that Winterson's narrator is a lesbian makes her better able to assume such a universal, that is, non-gender-marked position.[21] Although in some ways the fact that lesbians are women is inescapable (that is, after all, part of what makes them lesbians), lesbians are in many ways "not women," as Wittig succinctly puts it (32). Lesbian "is beyond the categories of sex (woman and man), because the designated subject 'lesbian' is *not* a woman, either economically, politically, or ideologically. For what makes a woman is a specific social relation to a man" (20). This distance of lesbians from womanhood by virtue of their distance from men may explain the amount of attention paid to Louise's husband, Elgin, in the novel.[22] It is only by understanding him that we can understand Louise's leaving him for the narrator.

It is important that we read Winterson's "concealment" of her narrator's gender and not just read through it by attempting to read the gender that is presumably concealed.[23] Winterson's refusal to mark the narrator's gender must be read as a strategy: what she attains through de-gendering the narrative voice is a universal subject position. As a "universal" voice, however, doesn't this narrator speak as a man, a possible result of the universalization of women and lesbians that Wittig doesn't consider?[24] As is well known, much of the work of feminism over the past twenty-five years has been aimed at particularizing one's position as subject and speaker. Concurrent with this is the critique of the masculine hidden under the guise of the universal. While I argue that the narrator of *Written on the Body* is feminine, I also argue that she is feminine under the guise of the universal/masculine. Such an impersonation is both disturbing, because it seems retrogressive, and exciting, because it seems subversive and productive. Again, my dual perspective here is informed by both Irigaray and Wittig. For Irigaray, if a woman were to adopt a masculine position, this would be disturbing because it further eradicates the feminine, the other sex, and bolsters the masculine, the one sex. For Wittig, however, a woman's adoption of a masculine position would be liberating because it would relieve woman of the burden of sex, by which she is always marked. If we consider not just the gender-less voice of the novel but what that voice is saying at various times, we might be able to escape this critical impasse. Early in the narrative, when the narrator has just entered her relationship with Louise, she seems to speak from a masculine position: she is

a Lothario, a rake who brags about the many women she has "had."
After she leaves Louise and begins to doubt herself and admit her
failure, her vulnerability positions her as a woman in the traditional sense. The flexible ego boundaries that the narrator discovers while with Louise also indicate a classically feminine subject
position. If the narrator can be and is both these things, isn't her
gender more nuanced than the simple designation "masculine"
or "feminine" would allow? I am tempted to say that, like Bernard,
the narrator moves from the masculine to the feminine end of the
gender spectrum. Yet, when the other characters analyzed here—
Robin, Matthew, V, and J—are also considered, the very fluidity of
their sex/gender identifications throws into question the metaphor of a "gender spectrum." A linear metaphor does not begin to
suggest the complexity of "other sexes."

AFTERWORD

For the category of sex is a totalitarian one . . . It shapes the
mind as well as the body since it controls all mental production. It grips our minds in such a way that we cannot
think outside of it. That is why we must destroy it and
start thinking beyond it if we want to start thinking at all,
as we must destroy the sexes as a sociological reality if we
want to start to exist.
                              —Monique Wittig, *The Straight Mind*

This epigraph from Monique Wittig originally served as the epigraph to the preface rather than the conclusion and this move is
significant. Why don't Wittig's theories work in my preface and
why do they work in my afterword? I would like to consider this
briefly, by way of concluding, since it says a good deal about what
I hope to have achieved in this book. I originally saw in Wittig's
belief that we need to destroy the sexes the natural conclusion to
the process that begins with an opening up of the gender binary
to the notion of "other sexes." But I felt I needed to temper Wittig's
call for moving beyond gender by fully considering what Luce
Irigaray suggests in the epigraph I used in Wittig's place—namely,
the idea that "if one day we are to be one [we must] now be *two*"
(*Sexes and Genealogies* 179). Irigaray's vision of the future of sexual
difference (being one) is quite different from Wittig's (being beyond).
Although I lean toward Irigaray's vision, at the same time I am
tempted by Wittig's vision, since it suggests the full-scale undoing
of gender as we know it, and I believe that Woolf's "other sexes"
leaves room for this possibility.

Here I will be only tracing Wittig's argument in *The Straight*

149

Mind in comparison to some of the central ideas of my study. While Irigaray contends that the masculine is the only sex, a concept that informs this study, Wittig, by contrast, sees woman as the only sex because she is always marked by sex (*The Straight Mind* 8).[1] Another way of saying this is that the category of sex designates women only, not men. As a result, women are doomed to take the limited, restricted place of the particular, while men enjoy the status of the universal subject (60). For Wittig, "gender . . . must be destroyed" (81), because it is under the name of gender (what Wittig usually refers to as "the category of sex") that oppression operates. As Wittig writes, "It is oppression that creates sex and not the contrary" (2). Only through dismantling the structure of difference is it possible to end oppression. In other words, difference or opposition does not reflect an already existing state of oppression but, rather, creates it.[2] For Wittig, the system of compulsory heterosexuality must be dismantled as well, because it is deeply entwined with the category of sex, which "founds society as heterosexual" (5). Unlike Irigaray, who advances an ethical relation between the sexes as the potential site of genuine sexual difference, Wittig rejects the heterosexual relation completely and bases much of her theory on the lesbian. The lesbian is a being outside or beyond the category of sex (20, 32). Wittig claims that "lesbians are not women"; hence, lesbians are not marked by gender, nor are they limited to the particular as the opposite of men.[3] On the one hand, I believe that the liberatory potential of this way of thinking is exciting, if not breathtaking, in its possibilities; however, I have to note that it is also faintly disturbing. Doing away with the category of sex entails a certain risk and is, moreover, nearly inconceivable. On the other hand, we might see in Wittig's argument that the category of sex must be eradicated the theoretical version of the textual dissolution of the genders that takes place in Hauser's and Winterson's novels. Wittig's lesbian who is not a woman could be described as "other-sexed" in the sense in which I have been discussing it here.

I ended my study with Winterson, for in its focus on gender and sexuality—the foundations of difference—and its challenging of the binary, *Written on the Body* brings together many of the manifestations of difference that I have analyzed throughout this study. In *The Waves*, masculine and feminine languages and identities are oppositionally defined and then brought together, in a move that resembles Irigaray's concept of the sensible transcendental. In *Nightwood*, the uncertain, undecidable nature of the third sex finds its home in the night, the space where anonymity prevails over identity. *The Talking Room* uses the mouth, the angel, the female body, and the sexually ambiguous in order to represent the otherness of the feminine. These various boundary crossings may be understood on different levels. Spatially, the night and the angel's other world are places that facilitate or propagate fluid boundaries. On the level of identity, all the novels trace a movement from a masculine, bounded, ego-based identity to a feminine, fluid identity. On a linguistic level, *The Waves* involves a reintegration of different languages; *Nightwood* deploys the chiasmus in order to concretize the issue of crossing; and *The Talking Room* uses punning and linguistic excess to mirror the gender and sexual excesses of its characters. Finally, the genderless narrative voice of *Written on the Body* attempts to reinscribe the feminine and the lesbian as the authoritative and universal. In terms of sex/gender, "other sexes" predominate over discrete masculine and feminine identities in each novel: Bernard's position as a feminine man and Matthew's "third-sexed" figures of inverts, dolls, and princes are modernist questionings of binary gender. J, whose sex, gender, sexual practice, and desire are seemingly conflicting and contradictory, and *Written on the Body*'s narrator's position as a lesbian whose gender is not revealed stand as postmodernist rejections of binary gender. In every case, these texts insist upon the "otherness" of sex, the complexity and excess of sex, and its refusal to be contained in binary terms.

According to Woolf in the epigraph to my preface, in order to find these traces of "other sexes," we need to travel to other worlds. The texts studied here, from Woolf to Winterson, Irigaray to Wittig, suggest by contrast that "other sexes" are plentiful in this world. What allows these women writers to see beyond binary sex is that they seek out what has been overlooked—the feminine element in all its associations—and not only reinstate it but make it central. Such a return of the repressed and repudiated feminine is a revolutionary move that allows us to see difference anew.

NOTES

Preface

1. I use the terms sex and gender somewhat interchangeably because I am proposing that the sex/gender distinction, which has taken hold in much feminist theory of the last ten years, must be questioned. Only by exploring the abundant connections between alternative sexualities and genders are we likely to begin dismantling the limiting binaries that still structure our thought on these issues. See chapter 1 for background on this debate.

2. Because most readers will not be familiar with Hauser, I have included references to a few of her major works in the "Works Cited."

3. Karl Heinrich Ulrichs was the first to develop this concept of homosexuality, which came to be known as "the third sex." This concept was further theorized and popularized by sexologists such as Richard von Krafft-Ebing and Havelock Ellis. See J. E. Rivers 265–66. Shari Benstock provides important commentary on the effects of such theories in the sociocultural realm for women writers of the 1920s and 1930s. See 49–52.

4. While "the third sex," as a combination of masculine and feminine, suggests the concept of androgyny, the ambiguously gendered "third sex" must be distinguished from the common notion of androgyny as a transcendence of gender. See Pamela Caughie, "Virginia Woolf's Double Discourse" 46, 51.

5. Because the system of binary gender works to obscure and conceal the feminine, rather than to reveal it, the feminine is the place where we must start in order to shake up the binary scheme for gender that constricts our thinking.

Chapter 1. (Re)placing the Feminine in Feminist Theory

1. This debate has its roots in Gayle Rubin's work from the early 1980s. In "The Traffic in Women," Rubin proposed that sex and gender be viewed as intertwined systems—as what she called the "sex/gender

system." Rubin defined this as "the set of arrangements by which a society transforms biological sexuality into products of human activity" (159). However, in a later article, Rubin proposed a distinction between sex and gender and this distinction took hold in a great deal of feminist theory. Rubin argued that "it is essential to separate gender and sexuality analytically to more accurately reflect their separate social existence" ("Thinking Sex" 308). Rubin's call for "an autonomous theory and politics specific to sexuality" ("Thinking Sex" 309) would seem to be answered by queer theorists of the 1990s like Eve Kosofsky Sedgwick. Sedgwick cites Rubin in detailing one of the "axioms" for her study *The Epistemology of the Closet*: "The study of sexuality is not coextensive with the study of gender; correspondingly, antihomophobic inquiry is not coextensive with feminist inquiry" (27). See 30 for Sedgwick's mention of Rubin.

2. Butler analyzes the way in which lesbian and gay studies positions itself as a discipline (represented by *The Lesbian and Gay Studies Reader*) by distancing itself from feminism and its purportedly exclusive focus on questions of gender ("Against Proper Objects" 1–7). Butler warns that to separate questions of sexuality from questions of sexual difference/gender will likely lead to two problems: the feminine will be placed on the side of the unrepresentable and a theory of sexuality that is divorced from gender will reproduce the masking of sexual difference that is typical of masculinist discourse (20). In other words, a theory of sexuality needs feminism in order to avoid repeating many of the problems of nonfeminist discourse.

3. Like Butler, Martin wants to keep the discourses on gender and sexuality in dialogue, but for slightly different reasons. She analyzes the way in which the feminine and the femme lesbian are often rendered invisible in queer discourse ("Sexualities without Genders" 108). When visible, the femme is typically portrayed as fixed, while other gender and sexual positions are privileged due to cross-gender identification (108, 119). Martin's account, like Butler's, points to the ways in which queer theory reenacts the worst features of phallocentric discourse due to this insistence on its distinction from feminism (or the distinction between gender and sex).

4. Irigaray elaborates her concept of mimesis in *This Sex Which Is Not One*. Although originally published in France in 1976, the English translation did not appear until 1985, making its reception in the United States contemporaneous with the works of Jardine and Spivak that I discuss here.

5. See *Gynesis* 72 for a complete list of "feminine" attributes. For an analysis of Aristotle's table of opposites in the *Metaphysics*, see Wittig 49–50.

6. *Gynesis*'s cover shows a painting in which a man dressed in shirt and tie stands stiffly next to what appears to be his self-portrait, but the figure in the painting is a nude woman.

7. See Sharon Willis's review of *Gynesis* for commentary on the limits of Jardine's "oedipal configuration" of the relation between female and male writers in France (33, 41).

8. Jardine writes, "Women cannot be thought of as somehow having been excluded from the symbolic; 'woman' cannot be given priority as panacea; nor can the articulation between women and woman go unthought" (48). Although Willis argues that Jardine lives up to these claims, she also points out that Jardine does not address the political and social differences between women (36). In other words, Jardine's emphasis falls on woman to the exclusion of women. In another review, Carol-Anne Tyler also simultaneously problematizes and insists on this woman-women connection (106). That this issue produces so many disclaimers and defenses points to both its importance and its difficulty.

9. For example, in her reading of Derrida, Jardine seeks to demonstrate that writing is a "feminine operation" (183) and that writing is "feminine in its essence." This is a difficult claim to make regarding any privileged Derridean term like writing, for Derrida sees writing, the trace, and différance as being outside of metaphysics (*Of Grammatology* 65). This is another way of saying that the feminine is inscribed in his texts as writing, a term privileged under many names and in many forms in his body of work. While writing in Derrida and the feminine in Irigaray do share certain attributes and occupy a similar place in their respective systems, they simply are not the same terms. A further problem with Jardine's reading of Derrida is that she takes terms that are explicitly feminine, such as the hymen, and reads them as being gender-free (191). And yet, it is precisely with such terms that the connection to women should be insisted upon. I will do so in my reading of the interview "Choreographies," in which Derrida comments on the hymen. See also "Women in the Beehive" 194–95.

10. Butler's *Bodies That Matter* warns about the error of construing matter or the body as irreducible. See chapter 1, especially 29–30.

11. Spivak defines phallogocentrism and phallocentrism in this way: "a structure of argument centered on the sovereignty of the engendering self and the determinacy of meaning (phallogocentrism); a structure of the text centered on the phallus as the determining moment (phallocentrism) or signifier" ("Displacement" 70).

12. See note 10.

13. Traditional ideas about the feminine are precisely what allow mimesis to operate in a subversive fashion. Irigaray's mimesis involves

what Jardine calls "obligatory connotations" of woman, and yet, unlike gynesis, it is a feminist operation.

14. Irigarayan mimesis must also be distinguished from other forms of mimesis such as unself-conscious "masquerade," which resembles Joan Riviere's formulation, or self-conscious "canny mimicry," which does not directly challenge the discourse of misogyny (Schor 48). Irigaray's version of mimesis is instead "a joyful reappropriation of the attributes of the other that is not in any way to be confused with a mere reversal of the existing phallocentric distribution of power" (Schor 48). For other feminist discussions of mimesis and masquerade, see Mary Ann Doane, "Film and the Masquerade" 81–82 and Butler, *Gender Trouble* 47–53.

15. For Spivak, displacement involves a violent appropriation of something that belongs to woman in a fundamental way. Yet she also finds it troubling that "the woman who is the 'model' for deconstructive discourse remains a woman generalized and defined in terms of the fake orgasm and other varieties of denial" (170). I would remark, however, that the fact that this woman calls to mind such overworked notions of womanhood points to a feminine remainder or excess that is not fully accounted for in the model of displacement.

16. In my reading of Matthew in *Nightwood*, for example, I claim that despite the complexity of Matthew's theoretical models, which foreground the ambiguity of "the third sex," Matthew believes in essential gender differences. Is this the case with Matthew, or is this perhaps an imposition of my lingering belief in fundamental gender differences, which may inform my reading not only of Matthew's understanding of gender but also my reading of the final chapter of the novel? Matthew, as a male mediator and authority, must be cleared away so that Nora and Robin can reach an understanding of themselves and their love for each other. Such an interpretation rests on the assumption that a man, even a transvestite "bearded lady," cannot know women as women can.

17. On the "dissonance" created by certain gender acts, see Butler, *Gender Trouble* 31, 137, 146. In other words, drag calls into question the idea of the congruence between sex, gender, sexual practice, and desire by signifying such gender identities as male sex, feminine gender, and male homosexual desire and practice.

18. My reading of Wittig differs from Butler's. It seems to me that Wittig does advocate going beyond gender: she writes that "gender . . . must be destroyed" (8, 81). Given Wittig's language, "transcendence" seems too mild a term to describe her goals.

19. For various glosses on the sensible transcendental, see Margaret Whitford *Luce Irigaray* 149, 164, 167; *The Irigaray Reader* 117.

20. The heterosexual basis of Irigaray's later work is made clear in

the first essay of *An Ethics,* where she expresses her concern for the rarity of "a nontraditional, fecund encounter between the sexes" (6) or "a relationship between two loving subjects of different sexes" (12).

21. For the angel, see *An Ethics* 15–16, 35–39, 42–46; *Sexes and Genealogies* 200. For the mucus, see *An Ethics* 18, 109–11; *Sexes and Genealogies* 201. For the double lips, see *An Ethics* 18; *Sexes and Genealogies* 100–101, 115. For the sexual encounter, see *An Ethics* 185–217 and "Questions to Emmanuel Levinas." These terms will be discussed in detail in subsequent chapters. These figures do not appear as such in *The Waves* and *Nightwood*; however, *The Talking Room* is filled with figures of angels, lips, and mouths, and *Written on the Body* places great emphasis on flesh, which is related to the mucus. The angel also appears in Winterson's novel.

Chapter 2. "This difference . . . this identity . . . was overcome"

1. Woolf also draws attention to the crossing of the boundary between linguistic and nonlinguistic in order to consider another issue that is central to the text—how to achieve some sense of control over the chaos and the terror that life represents. For Eric Warner, this is a central concern of the novel: "Life has no shape, but the human need to find one is omnipresent: this is the 'essential' paradox to which *The Waves* is committed" (104).

2. The reintegration of masculine and feminine that I am describing here is related to androgyny, but should not be confused with it. Androgyny involves a stable union, or even blurring, of masculine and feminine, while, in my figures of "other sexes," difference is fully achieved, or heightened. For an example of the use of androgyny to signify the blurring of genders, see Ellen Bayuk Rosenman. Androgyny is a recurrent theme in the history of Woolf criticism (for a review, see Mark Hussey, *Virginia Woolf A to Z* 3–6).

3. Criticism on *The Waves* tends to divide into two tendencies in terms of the reading of character and identity. Critics of the 1960s and 1970s tended to stress the union of the characters as well as the growth of identity. Critics of the 1980s and 1990s tended to stress the division of the characters as well as the destruction of identity. I will refer to both types of readings in the course of this chapter. Jean Guiguet argues that these two meetings bring about the formation of a "multiple consciousness" from the characters' linked identities. While I agree that the characters seek to escape identity at these meetings, I argue that they seek anonymity, not a "synthesis" with other identities (291). Like Guiguet, Alice Van Buren Kelley argues that the characters attain moments of "true communion" and "visionary unity" at both of their meetings: I would suggest

that these moments are glimpsed, but are severely undermined by the constructed nature of all identity, which prevents both "true" identity and a "true communion" of disparate identities (169, 187–88).

4. Garrett Stewart also notes Bernard's foundation of identity in and through language and Rhoda's inability to locate herself in language and her subsequent lack of identity (426–27, 434–36). However, his focus is on a phonic phenomenon that he calls "transegmental drift"—sound play between the final phonemes of words—which is outside the concerns of this study. Despite the gendered nature of subjectivity and language in *The Waves*, Stewart repeatedly effaces the category of gender from his discussion (442, 452, 455, 458). Stewart also postulates a universal subject that is problematic in the context of Woolf's work, as well as in his Kristevan reading of it (455).

5. Guiguet writes of the "multiple consciousness" or "synthesis" of the characters (291). James Naremore states that the "six disembodied voices" form "one observant spirit" (175). Maria DiBattista, on the other hand, makes a more convincing case that the "characters" should be considered "speaking voices" or "threshold beings" who, when taken together, "do not compose a satisfactory whole" (163). See note 3 above.

6. Two critics who have focused on the role of identity in the novel are Susan Dick and Avrom Fleishman. Dick argues that memory plays a key role in the formation of self, with the failure of memory causing self-loss in Bernard's summing up. I argue, on the other hand, that self-loss arises from the structure of identity itself. Like Dick, Fleishman focuses on Bernard's meditations on the subject of identity, but does not turn his attention to the destruction of selfhood that also preoccupies Bernard, as well as each of the other characters.

7. In her critique of the Edwardian novelists, Woolf argues that "life or spirit, truth or reality, this, the essential thing" is not "contained any longer in such ill-fitting vestments as we provide"—namely the plot and form of the realist novel ("Modern Fiction" 105). Woolf is attempting to show the way in which she and her more experimental contemporaries had to work against the constraints of outdated formal models. Like Joyce, Woolf was "concerned at all costs to reveal the flickerings of that innermost flame which flashes its messages through the brain" (107), and in *The Waves* it is the reunion of feminine and masculine languages that makes this possible.

8. Rachel Bowlby points out the characters' need to make connections, to establish sequence in order to keep identity together. She writes that Rhoda's "identity collapses" because of her failure to see sequence in the world about her (166). She also notes that Woolf frequently figures the writing process through images of consecutive movement such as

the walk in *A Room of One's Own* and the train ride in "Mr. Bennett and Mrs. Brown."

9. Yet fragments and stories depend upon each other: this is Bernard's final realization at the end of the novel. Bernard even acknowledges the usefulness of the biographic style, and what "it does to tack together torn bits of stuff" (259). Several things are interesting here: first, Bernard uses the image of sewing, which in the novel is associated with women, as I'll discuss below. Second, Woolf incorporates a positive reference to her father, Sir Leslie Stephen, editor of the *Dictionary of National Biography*.

10. Makiko Minow-Pinkney's Kristevan reading of the novel is a significant contribution to the criticism. Her chapter discusses the "anti-symbolic stance" of the novel. While my argument shares some territory— Rhoda's exclusion from the symbolic, Bernard's ambiguous gender (which Minow-Pinkney reads as "androgyny"), a focus on the little language— I question the use of Kristeva as a model for Woolf's work on subjectivity. Judith Butler's reading of Julia Kristeva's theory of the semiotic has strongly influenced my reading of the placement of the feminine in *The Waves*: "*Cultural* subversion is not really Kristeva's concern, for subversion, when it appears, emerges from beneath the surface of culture only inevitably to return there . . . By relegating the source of subversion to a site outside of culture itself, Kristeva appears to foreclose the possibility of subversion as an effective or realizable cultural practice. Pleasure beyond the paternal law can be imagined only together with its inevitable impossibility" (*Gender Trouble* 87–88; emphasis in original). See also 79–80, 82 for the development of this argument. Because the novel's disruptive forces come from within culture itself, they are more potentially disruptive. I also contend that the stark divisions that Woolf sets up are eventually complicated and confounded to a great degree. Thus, in reference to Minow-Pinkney's assertion that Rhoda is the exemplary feminine subject, excluded from the symbolic order (168–70), I would argue that since Rhoda speaks and even speaks about her "exclusion" from the symbolic, it is not quite accurate to say that she is simply alienated from the symbolic order. In the final analysis, even Bernard is in some sense alienated from the symbolic by the end of the novel, but still part of it.

11. In her lack of identity, Rhoda resembles Robin Vote in *Nightwood*, J in *The Talking Room*, and the nameless narrator in *Written on the Body*: this anonymity makes each a privileged figure.

12. In the similar scene at Percival's party, when it is also Louis who signals the breaking of the circle of union and the reassertion of their characters, he remarks, "Now the current flows. Now passions that lay in wait down there in the dark weeds which grow at the bottom rise and pound us with their waves" (142).

13. Ruth Porritt analyzes Woolf's radical "disarticulation of the self" in comparison to Derrida's tamer deconstruction of the self. While I find Porritt's argument compelling, I argue that Woolf's subject is gendered, and thus gender must be an essential component of the way we read Woolf's work on subjectivity. As I contend here, Bernard's self comes undone but is redone through his incorporation of feminine language and feminine subjectivity.

14. By making the "little language," which is associated only with women at this point, the language of activity and libido, Woolf rewrites the traditional association of femininity with passivity.

15. Susan Stanford Friedman's analysis of the use of lyric discourse as an oppositional strategy that disrupts linear narrative in *To the Lighthouse* sheds light on the function of the "little language" in *The Waves* (164–65, 171–75). Friedman compares these two discourses to the Kristevan semiotic and symbolic; in this way, her reading dovetails Minow-Pinkney's reading, discussed above (see Friedman 165–66).

16. In her essay "Craftsmanship" Woolf describes the interactions of words in a similar way: words "live in the mind . . . by ranging hither and thither, by falling in love and mating together" (250).

17. See Hussey, *The Singing of the Real World* 5–6.

18. Percival's connection to the world is even more unmediated than Susan's or Jinny's, and for this reason he is the silent and mostly absent hero of the novel, whom all the characters desire. Neville describes Percival's unmediated immersion in the world in this way: "Not a thread, not a sheet of paper lies between him and the sun, between him and the moon" (48). Like Susan, Percival plays the role of the silent muse, a typically feminine role: though barred from language, he inspires poetry. See also Neville's remarks on Percival and poetry on 40 and 48.

19. Susan here differs greatly from Jinny who uses the "little language" in order to unite with a man whom she desires in a passage discussed above.

20. As Susan ages, she begins to express her disgust with traditional femininity: "I am sick of the body, I am sick of my own craft, industry and cunning, of the unscrupulous ways of the mother." She longs for a "shadow," a "shock" to jar her out of her maternal ways, something related to Bernard's childhood stories and his image of the woman writing at Elvedon (191). It is a new connection to language—the masculine language of stories combined with women's writing—that would provide this shock. Similarly, Bernard does not simply trade stories for fragments or cries: he brings them together in a third possibility

21. Even in the early parts of the novel, Bernard is critical of the notion of individual identity when he is part of a mob of people. Such

mergings of the individual with an unknown group of people foster communion in a way that is impossible with his group of friends (111–12). What Bernard eventually discovers is that the turn away from individual identity now allows him to be a writer, a major shift in his thinking that begins to pave the way for his new understanding of the connection between writing and subjectivity in the "summing up." There, Bernard comes to the realization that displaced subjectivity will allow him access to the feminine language, a language more genuine than the false language of stories.

22. The many images of the waves within the text are an aspect of the novel that is unfortunately beyond the scope of this chapter. Taking the forms of the waves and the tide, water signifies abundantly, representing the mundane aspects of life, violent emotions, death, nothingness, and, in a self-reflexive fashion, as I discuss in a separate essay, the novel itself (see Harris).

23. The chant of "must, must, must" returns significantly at the very end of the novel, as Bernard, now "a man without a self," is about to face death (295–96).

24. Neville is included in this group of women because of his homosexuality, which means that he does not have the same association with conventional masculinity as Bernard and Louis do.

25. Bernard successfully brings forth this "stream" in a passage where he walks along the street, talking out loud, mixing children's rhymes with poetry: "mingling nonsense and poetry, floating in the stream" (282).

26. J. W. Graham has pointed out that Woolf's use of the pure present, an unusual tense for narration, "robs" the events "of their psychological substance, their felt duration *as actions*" ("Point of View in *The Waves*" 96).

27. See "Modern Fiction" 104–6.

28. In a separate essay, I extend this discussion of "the thing in itself" in *The Waves*, focusing in particular on Neville's discovery of the thing in itself through writing poetry (see Harris). For other critics who take up the issue from a phenomenological perspective, see Henke and McConnell. See also references in Warner (31, 103) and Miko (64).

29. While Bernard claims that he cannot speak, he continues to speak. His monologue does not stop; the novel does not end. Perhaps, then, it is more appropriate to say that he perceives a dramatic change for the worse in his linguistic abilities but does not necessarily experience it.

30. In another passage, Bernard uses a metaphor of inscription upon the earth to describe the process of acquiring an identity: "I became, I mean, a certain kind of man, *scoring my path across life* as one treads a path across the fields" (260; emphasis added).

31. Again, Bernard relies on the image of words as the veil that covers the things it designates, a figure he sometimes inverts so that words take the veil off things.

32. This type of intersubjective relationship is also found in *Written on the Body*.

33. Similar metaphors are used to describe Bernard's stories as well: Neville refers to his friend's "bit of string," which sags when his story is a failure (39).

34. It is worth noting that *The Waves* is much more *about* a feminine language of howls, cries, barks, and groans than it is comprised of these forms of vocalization. Bernard comes closer to a cry than any other character in his final words—"O Death!" (297)—yet even this cry is contained by the narrative voice of the interludes, which closes the text: *"The waves broke on the shore"* (emphasis in original). Finally, story seems to predominate over fragment. The "monotony" of the novel's language is frequently mentioned in the criticism, and one reason for this is the exclusively discursive nature of the characters' monologues.

35. Rhoda's suicide is anticipated in a passage in which she gazes down on the waves and imagines being immersed in them (205–6). Bernard also alludes to her suicide (266) and finally reports it (281, 288–89).

36. Bernard's ambiguous gender position in his "summing up" makes him a figure of the androgynous artist similar to Woolf's ideal in *A Room of One's Own* (100–108).

37. Masculine displacement, as analyzed in chapter 1, involves the privileging of qualities associated with femininity—the body, the unconscious, nonidentity—by the masculine subject who then appropriates the place of woman for his own. See Spivak's analysis of displacement in deconstruction in "Displacement and the Discourse of Woman" 169–73.

Chapter 3. "The Third Sex"

1. Given the fact that *Nightwood* is a modernist text, it may be that Matthew's femininity actually provides, rather than undercuts, his narrative authority. According to Spivak, as discussed in chapter 1, the masculine displacement of the feminine subject position provides deconstruction with its discursive power ("Displacement" 169–73). I read Matthew similarly as a male theorist who masquerades as woman in order to displace his own subjectivity.

2. Inversion is, in a sense, a predecessor of homosexuality. George Chauncey has examined the shift in terms around the turn of the century. Inversion referred more broadly to sex role and gender characteristics, while homosexuality began to be used at the time when the discourse on

sexuality shifted to a more narrow focus on identity (119). Although the sections on *Nightwood* that focus on inversion take place in the 1920s, when the shift to homosexuality had already been made, Barnes uses inversion, I contend, because she sees sexuality as interrelated with gender or sex role and as affecting behavior on many levels.

3. These figures must be read both thematically and stylistically, for issues of gender and style cannot be separated in the study of women modernists' texts where gender experimentation is tied closely to stylistic experimentation. Style was the primary focus of criticism on Barnes until the late 1980s when Sandra M. Gilbert and Susan Gubar, Shari Benstock, and Frann Michel brought attention to the centrality of gender within Barnes's texts, while also examining style. See Gilbert and Gubar, *Sexchanges*; Benstock, *Women of the Left Bank: Paris, 1900–1940*; and Michel, "Displacing Castration: *Nightwood, Ladies Almanack,* and Feminine Writing." One notable early study of gender and style in *Nightwood* is Carolyn Allen's 1978 essay "'Dressing the Unknowable in the Garments of the Known': The Style of Djuna Barnes's *Nightwood*." Recent feminist readings of the novel by Judith Lee and Jane Marcus that continue the study of gender and style appear in Mary Lynn Broe's *Silence and Power: A Reevaluation of Djuna Barnes*. In my focus on Matthew as a storyteller/theorist, I am returning to one of the tendencies of the Barnes criticism of the 1970s and early 1980s. The critics Charles Baxter, Elizabeth Pochoda, and Alan Singer, whose work I will examine below, tended to emphasize Matthew's discursive power and narrative authority, which they saw as eclipsing Barnes's authorial power. I would like to reread Matthew's narrative authority and the focus of his narrative—inversion and gender—in light of some of the insights of feminist Barnes studies on the text's inscription of gender.

4. For convincing readings of Robin as a representation of the feminine, see Michel 41–42 and Lee 210–11.

5. Allen was the first critic to recognize the subjects of *Nightwood* as "the power of the night, of irrationality and the unconscious; and the nature of love, particularly love between women" and to suggest the connection between the night and inversion. See "'Dressing the Unknowable'" 107.

6. My references are to the 1937 New Directions edition. My argument is based on this edition, rather than Cheryl J. Plumb's edition of the drafts, which appeared in 1995, because at the time this chapter was written, by far the majority of Barnes criticism was based on the 1937 edition.

7. See Irigaray's discussion of the masculine imaginary as focused on sameness (*This Sex* 28), and her insistence that women need to live out their otherness in opposition to sameness (205).

8. The style of "Watchman, What of the Night?" and "Go Down, Matthew" resembles that of *The Waves*. The two texts are comprised of long stretches of recorded speech: characters are speaking, but the characters are not speaking to each other. The effect is that of drama, with characters delivering soliloquies. The language, which is dense and heavily metaphorical, is also more suited to soliloquy than to dialogue.

9. In these passages on the need to think the night and day as one, we see the refusal of opposition. Allen notes that semantically opposed terms are often linked syntactically in the text ("'Dressing the Unknowable'" 113). Allen reads this tendency as a sign of Barnes's refusal to "acknowledge [the] dichotomous tensions" between opposites that "are so bound up in each other that duality is impossible" (113).

10. In *Bodies That Matter*, Butler problematizes the relationship between sex and gender. In this text, Butler critiques the familiar account of gender "as a cultural construction which is imposed upon the surface of matter, understood either as 'the body' or its given sex" (2). Instead, she rejects the notion of sex as "simple fact or static condition of the body" (2) and analyzes the construction of sex as matter. Her new question, then, is, "[T]hrough what regulatory norms is sex itself materialized?" (10). In my reading of *Nightwood*, I focus primarily on gender and sexuality as intertwined. Barnes tends to see sex as fixed, as "simple fact," but at times her destabilization of gender and sexuality carries over to sex as well.

11. While Robin rebels against both pregnancy and motherhood, in some sense rejecting her gender role, her possibilities for complete rejection are more limited than those of Matthew, who rebels against masculinity through dressing as a woman. Matthew can refuse to engage in heterosexual, masculine sexual behavior, while Robin's reproductive capacity is a constant fact of life.

12. Gender role is defined as "a set of expectations about what behaviors are appropriate for people of one gender" (Kessler and McKenna 11).

13. On the denaturalization of gender in drag performance, see Esther Newton 103, 107.

14. Marcus comments on Matthew as a scathing parody of Freud, or of sexologists in general (233–34, 245). For discussions of the masculine displacement of the feminine subject position, see note 1, above, as well as chapter 1.

15. See note 17, below.

16. See the discussion of mimesis, a term closely related to masquerade, in chapter 1.

17. In another scene, Matthew again "plays" a woman in private. In

"La Somnambule," after reviving Robin from her faint, he applies her makeup and perfume, an act that Felix happens to catch (36). Of his method of applying lipstick, Barnes notes that he presses his lips together "in order to have it seem that their sudden embellishment was a visitation of nature" (36). Clearly, even in the midst of the masquerade, Matthew wishes to appear to be "natural."

18.   Pochoda writes that "[t]he novel has already jettisoned language; O'Connor has exited, and really there is no way to rescue the end of the story from the melodrama it has eschewed so far" (188). The style of "The Possessed" is spare and monosyllabic not because Barnes has reached her limit in previous chapters, but because language has been such an obstacle to Robin and Nora that they attempt silence as a last resort. Moreover, the novel's resources are not depleted; rather, Matthew's resources are depleted because the misery that he experiences in telling stories on subjects that others are "keeping hushed" leads him to choose silence over speech as well (162).

19.   Yet some critics, like Baxter, see in Matthew a masterful prophet (1180). Baxter's traditional view of masculine authority would be undercut completely were he to acknowledge Matthew's femininity. Ignoring this, Baxter depicts him as a figure of monolithic authority, a prophet, a character who steals the novel.

20.   For a discussion of the masculine/feminine hierarchy, see Hélène Cixous, "Sorties" 90–91. My discussion of the status of the masculine/ feminine opposition in *Nightwood* is informed by Michel's convincing argument that the feminine in Barnes's texts closely resembles the feminine within the work of Hélène Cixous, Luce Irigaray, and Julia Kristeva. See Michel 34–39.

21.   Butler's notion of the relation between stable gender and destabilizing gender provides a clear framework for Barnes's notion of the third sex as I am formulating it here: gender is destabilized "through the mobilization, subversive confusion, and proliferation of precisely those constitutive categories that seek to keep gender in its place by posturing as the foundational illusions of identity" (*Gender Trouble* 34).

22.   Matthew's transvestism is in keeping with his use of nineteenth-century terms for the homosexual. Chauncey notes that in the Victorian era, transvestism was "seen as characteristic of inversion" (119), but in the modern era, Havelock Ellis and others distinguished homosexuality from transvestism, which was then associated primarily with heterosexual men (122).

23.   See Butler, *Gender Trouble* 136–38 for a reading of drag as a subversive practice that creates gender confusion and proliferation.

24.   My reading of these figures owes much to Andrzej Warminski's

reading of an asymmetrical chiasmus in Nietzsche's *The Birth of Tragedy* (xxxv–lxi). The metaphor in question that undergoes a chiasmic reversal involves the opposition of Apollo and Dionysos, light and dark, blinding and healing. Warminski's text dwells on this figure for some thirty pages and cannot be paraphrased here. However, the thrust of his reading is that Apollonian light is found to result in the same nothingness that the Dionysian night presents to the senses. And this nothing is "radically unknowable" in terms of binary opposition. This is the reason for the figure's bursting the boundaries of a tidy symmetrical reversal. I would suggest that similarly, for Barnes, gender and sexuality cannot be contained or even suggested within the confines of a scheme of thinking based on binary opposition.

25. See Michel 42, for a convincing gloss on this passage. She points out that the female invert "contains the difference that she is"—the difference of inversion—while the male invert "becomes an invert by containing the difference of the feminine." According to Michel, Matthew's figures of inversion thus reaffirm the gender binary in that difference is located "on the side of Woman" in these figures. Yet Michel argues that another of Matthew's descriptions of the invert "disrupt[s]" the "binary structure of gender" (42). She reads the description of the invert as "neither one and half the other" as stressing otherness and difference, and thus disrupting the gender binary (*Nightwood* 136). While I agree that Matthew's figures rely on the gender binary to a certain degree, I argue that the asymmetry of the figures, as well as the complex interplay among all components of gender identity in the text's inverts—sex, gender, sexual practice, and desire—result in the disruption rather than the reaffirmation of the gender binary.

26. While Robin's androgyny is described as a natural trait, it is also deliberate in that she dresses like a boy, perhaps to enhance her masculinity.

27. The idea of Robin as a man trapped in a woman's body is put forward by Gilbert and Gubar, but it is an idea that the language of the text does not bear out. See *Sexchanges* 216–17. As I've noted above, Matthew does see himself as a woman trapped in a man's body.

28. On "the third sex," see the preface, note 3.

29. In a response to Robin's refusal of love, Nora displaces her love to a stand-in, the doll. Nora in this way resembles the melancholiac of Freud's "Mourning and Melancholia," as does B in *The Talking Room* ("Mourning and Melancholia" 164–66). Butler's reading of the incorporative structure of melancholy in the formation of gender identity is also suggestive in relation to Nora, but this issue is too involved to take up adequately in this chapter. See Butler, *Gender Trouble* 48–53.

30. This is but one of a series of metaphors in *Nightwood* that involve the joining and merging of halves and that indicate the overcoming of opposition. See 38, 69, 138.

31. Not only does Barnes subvert the opposition of masculine and feminine by means of this metaphor of the face, but she also subverts the opposition of spirit and body, an opposition that is congruent with the masculine/feminine opposition. For the face is seen as conveying identity, and yet it is a part of the body: it conjoins the internal (the soul) and the external (the body) on the level of the body.

32. On the question of the relation of heterosexuality and homosexuality to gender identity, Butler writes that "[t]he replication of heterosexual constructs in non-heterosexual frames brings into relief the utterly constructed status of the so-called heterosexual original. Thus, gay is to straight *not* as copy is to original, but, rather, as copy is to copy. The parodic repetition of 'the original' . . . reveals the original to be nothing other than a parody of the *idea* of the natural and the original" (*Gender Trouble* 31; emphasis in original). This de-naturalization of the so-called natural basis of gender and sexuality (their supposed basis in anatomical sex) through parody and mimicry is what is behind the placement of the prince, the doll, and the invert in the realm of fiction. Fiction, like mimicry and parody, is in the register of rhetoric and performance.

33. Marcus analyzes "the body of the Other—the black, lesbian, transvestite, or Jew—presented as text in the novel" and relates this to Barnes's critique of Fascist and Nazi politics in the 1930s (221).

Chapter 4. *"A Secret Second Tongue"*

1. *The Talking Room*, although continuously in print since 1976, has yet to gain wide readership and critical recognition. This picture may be changing: Ewa Ziarek's article, the first thorough reading of the novel, attempts to situate the text in the dialogue on feminism and postmodernism. Ziarek reads the novel in terms of Kristeva's theory of the semiotic and argues that the narrative involves a search for the "maternal source of language" that exceeds the simple notion of origin and must be thought instead in terms of translation (498–99). Ellen G. Friedman and Miriam Fuchs discuss Hauser in their overview of women experimentalists and situate her in the third generation of this tradition (7, 31–32, 311). Robert L. Caserio examines the novel in the context of public/private debates about sodomy and homosexual parenting. Larry McCaffery and Sinda Gregory's interviews with Hauser provide biographical sketches and a discussion of her writing practice. Apart from these articles, Hauser has received some praise from various reviewers

and commentators for her stylistic achievements (on the irony of these reviews, given the continued neglect of her work, see Ziarek 480–82).

2. While these three main characters and the other lesbians they encounter are named only with initials, other minor characters are given full names: these are granny-anny, V's mother; Flo, V's African American maid; and Olli, B's boyfriend. By creating this pronounced difference in naming, Hauser seems to be ascribing in-group status to the lesbian characters and out-group status to the other characters. The initials also serve to destabilize the notion of identity in the broad sense, which is a function of the destabilization of gender identity.

3. See Ziarek 490 for a discussion of V's investment in the values of property, propriety, and legitimacy.

4. See 14 where she regales J, who barely pays attention, with the tale of "the agonies [she] endured!" during one of her search and rescue missions to locate J.

5. B also sees the O as the empty circle, which she associates with her unborn child: "As yet no sex or name tag for my baby and O will have to do till I know more. O is a blank I can fill in with any shape or face I like" (153). Similarly, identity is a "blank I can fill in" for the characters of the novel. Ziarek notes that the O of the mirror frame that B also mentions is a metaphor for her future text (500).

6. The similarities between *The Talking Room* and *Nightwood* are striking, particularly the connections between J and Robin Vote. Both drinkers and wanderers whose sexuality and gender are fluid and undecidable, neither woman can conjure up a story of her whereabouts for her frantic lover. The scene in which J vaguely recalls kneeling on the floor with a dog in a stranger's bedroom seems like a direct reference to the final scene of *Nightwood*, in which Robin crawls on the floor of the chapel with Nora's dog (*The Talking Room* 143; *Nightwood* 170).

7. In the text's suspension of the referential function of language, its postmodern style becomes evident, and this postmodernism is based in the novel's particular conception of the feminine. See Pamela L. Caughie's discussion of the reference theory of language with respect to postmodernism in *Virginia Woolf and Postmodernism* 8, 14, 79. Caughie ties Woolf's notion of androgyny to her challenging of the referential function of language (see also her essay "Virginia Woolf's Double Discourse" 44–45). I would argue that the same sort of connection is at work in Hauser.

8. Ziarek analyzes the idea of origin in reference to B's search for her mother, while my discussion of origin here is primarily aimed at the novel's style. As for B's relationship to her mother, I tend to emphasize instead the erotic nature of this love.

9. See *The Talking Room* 28, 71, 142.

10. In her bigness and her pregnancy, which coincide with her pubescence, B is a figure of the grotesque body, a figure closely associated with the discourse of masquerade, as Mary Russo has demonstrated. Russo's notion of the grotesque body comes from Mikhail Bakhtin: "The grotesque body is the open, protruding, extended, secreting body, the body of becoming, process, and change" (219). One can see this in B's fascination with her body and its changes as she goes through pregnancy. Russo notes that although the woman as the embodiment of the grotesque body has negative connotations, "the hyperboles of masquerade and carnival suggest, at least, some preliminary 'acting out' of the dilemmas of femininity" (225).

11. Dilatory style involves extension, delay, and generation of more narrative. These narrative qualities are attained not only through style but also through plot tricks such as pregnancy, which not only delays the ending but also expands the plot's (and the pregnant character's) contours through the production of another character (Parker 19).

12. According to Irigaray, not only is the inside/outside opposition undermined by the lips but also related spatial oppositions: "Our depth is the thickness of our body, our all touching itself. Where top and bottom, inside and outside, in front and behind, above and below are not separated, remote, out of touch. Our all intermingled. Without breaks or gaps" (*This Sex* 213).

13. Judith Roof writes that the lesbian "conveys a different, concerted absence which frustrates both symmetry and visibility" (101). See also her discussion of the way in which the hidden (or, secret, for Hauser) nature of the source of lesbian desire (Woolf's "match in the crocus") breaks from phallic representation (114).

14. Irigaray also views woman's mouth as mysterious or secret. See the second epigraph to this chapter.

15. See Paula Bennett's analysis of clitoral imagery in the work of Emily Dickinson and other nineteenth-century American women poets, which cites the "jewel" as a recurring clitoral image (236). Bennett's argument about the symptomatic failure of feminist literary criticism and feminist psychoanalytic theory to seriously consider the clitoris is a powerful one. She calls for a "construction of female sexuality that takes the clitoris centrally into account" so that we may see women as autonomous agents of their own sexuality (256). Hauser's novel is daring in its depiction of many facets of lesbian sexuality, especially the clitoris and the tongue.

16. Seeds are also mentioned by Bennett as a form of clitoral imagery in nineteenth-century women's poetry (243).

17. B's relationship to J as well as her orality might be understood as

a type of melancholic identification and incorporation. In "Mourning and Melancholia," Freud notes the role of cannibalistic incorporation in melancholia. In response to a loss, the libido is "withdrawn" into the ego instead of being displaced onto another object, as in mourning. The ego then identifies with the original object in a form of "narcissistic identification." The mechanism whereby the identification takes place is the following: "[T]he ego wants to incorporate this object into itself, and in accordance with the oral or cannibalistic phase of libidinal development in which it is, it wants to do so by devouring it" (171; see also "Three Essays on Sexuality" 198). Freud also notes that the melancholiac's oral fixation often manifests itself in the "refusal of nourishment" ("Mourning and Melancholia" 171), and Irigaray, who defines melancholia as a typically feminine disorder, refers to the connection between anorexia and the young girl's refusal of her sexual "blossoming" (*Speculum* 69). In B's case, her refusal of femininity manifests itself in eating, rather than in refusing to eat.

18.   Flo's mouth is at least doubly other in the framework of dominant, masculinist culture, which relies for its functioning on racism as much as on misogyny or heterosexism. Because V endorses such a framework, her reaction to Flo's mouth is horror, whereas her reaction to J's mouth is attraction. B also dwells on the mouth of granny-anny, her Croatian grandmother, who, like Flo, is a maid. In Flo and granny-anny, feminine otherness (J's otherness) is magnified: they are triply other as women, minorities, and working-class servants. See 86–88 for the scene where granny-anny makes a spectacle of her mouth for V and her friends.

19.   V also admits that she has had "nightmares" in which Flo's tongue transformed into her ex-husband's (Jock's) penis: "[H]er horrid tongue was all over and into me, it changed, Jesus, it became Jake or Jock, Jock's you know what" (37). J responds openly to the sexualized nature of this scene. When V tells her of "Flo's walrus tongue . . . Huge, pink and slimy," J says "Sounds yummy to me" (37).

20.   See Irigaray, *Sexes and Genealogies* 100–101; *An Ethics of Sexual Difference* 18. Because the lips also confound opposition and dichotomy, they are another figure of the between such as Woolf's "little language," Barnes's "the third sex," and Winterson's bodily writing.

21.   I am using Judith Butler's definition of gender identity as "a relationship among sex, gender, sexual practice, and desire" (*Gender Trouble* 18). Suzanne J. Kessler and Wendy McKenna's definition of "gender identity" has also influenced my use of the term: they define it as an "individual's own feeling of whether she or he is a woman or a man" or "self-attribution of gender" (8).

22.   On gender as an imitative structure, see Esther Newton 103; Kessler and McKenna 113; Butler, *Gender Trouble* 24–25, 112.

23. Butler remarks on the categories of original and copy in the relation between heterosexual/gay identities: "The replication of heterosexual constructs in non-heterosexual frames brings into relief the utterly constructed status of the so-called heterosexual original. Thus, gay is to straight *not* as copy is to original, but, rather, as copy is to copy" (*Gender Trouble* 31).

24. Being neither a woman nor a man, J is clearly an other-sexed figure, like Robin Vote in *Nightwood*. See chapter 3 for a similar discussion of Robin.

25. According to V, a butch lesbian like J is simply not a woman, as is plain from her suspicions about the motive behind J's desire to conceive a child "naturally"—by sleeping with a man. Yet several passages in the novel, which I will examine below, put into question V's status as a woman as well, leaving the possibility that femmes are not women either.

26. Referring to hysterectomy as castration signals the secondary nature of female sexuality in normative frameworks.

27. This is a notion that Butler explores in *Gender Trouble*, but fully addresses in *Bodies That Matter*, which examines the "construction" of sex and matter.

28. In this way, V's wish resembles the concept of gender coherence by which the compulsory regime of heterosexuality legitimizes itself, according to Butler. In other words, gender is conceived as "a unity of experience, of sex, of gender and desire" (*Gender Trouble* 22; see also 31–32). V's marriage fantasy functions in the same way: it would create order out of disorder, unity out of multiplicity.

29. Not surprisingly, D's longing for a return to clear-cut gender distinctions is tied to his longing for a return to the institutionalized oppression and containment of women. He "longs for the mauve era when a lady's face was swathed in veils and . . . she would sit . . . immobilized by whalebone stays . . . Ah, for the hourglass waist!" (50).

30. See *The Talking Room* 67. The line from Rilke is from the second "Duino Elegy" 13.

31. Ziarek also reads J's unwritten poems as relating to B's own creativity, yet she sees the blank page of the poems more as a potential space rather than the narrative that she is already writing, that is, *The Talking Room*, which is how I discuss it here. See 499–500.

32. B is certain that J does not know German, but copies the line letter by letter. She has probably borrowed the Rilke volume from Q, a woman with whom she is having an affair (68). Q does speak German; therefore, J may know the meaning of lines from Q. Perhaps Q, like V, calls J her "terrible angel" as well.

33. V also calls her angel on other occasions (59, 60, 63), and B makes

a similar reference in a passage that I will examine below (155). By citing Rilke's naming of the angel as terrifying, J may also be commenting on her lover's attempt to capture her within an identity that she finds confining.

34.   While my reading of the angel hinges on Irigaray's angel, Ziarek's reading focuses on Rilke's angel, who "liberates himself from the order of the visible by the act of spiritual transformation" (497).

35.   Irigaray quotes the same line from Rilke that J quotes (*Sexes and Genealogies* 39).

36.   Elizabeth Grosz comments on the angel in Irigaray: "The angel traverses distinct identities and categories to foretell the union of differences, particularly the union of the sexes in marriage, conception and birth, announcing sexual productivity and exchange. The angel thus represents the divine union of the sexes, without, significantly, having a sex of its own" (161). In a system of binary gender, the angel may not have a sex; but if we look beyond such a system, the angel could be said to possess an other sex, a sex beyond the categories masculine and feminine. This sense is conveyed in the continuation of Grosz's passage: angels "signify the possibility of a bridge between . . . male and female." But "they are usually disembodied, sexually neuter, intangible, incorporeal. They move between one order and other while being identified with neither. They are thus able to act as ideals of a meeting or middle ground between the sexes" (161).

37.   This passage sheds light as well on J's book of unwritten poems. Herself a text, how would J, the angel, write? J shrinks back from the blank pages of the book, for how would she write her own emptiness—her silence, her mystery, her anonymity, her animality, her wandering? Yet, she does suggest meaning, like the angel in the passage, whose words are "inaudible . . . unheard . . . invisible."

38.   See Irigaray, *This Sex*, "The 'Mechanics' of Fluids."

Chapter 5. A Feminist Ethics of Love

1.   The gender of Winterson's first-person narrator is never specified in the text, a fact that has been widely discussed in reviews of the novel. In the few critical essays on Winterson, this issue has not been adequately resolved, I would argue. I refer to the narrator as "she" throughout this chapter because there is much support, both textual and extratextual, for reading "it" as a "her." I will discuss this in detail later in the chapter.

2.   In a note to Irigaray's essay "The Limits of the Transference," Margaret Whitford provides a gloss on the sensible transcendental: "The sensible transcendental is a term which refers to the overcoming of the split between material and ideal, body and spirit, immanence and tran-

scendence, and their assignment to women and men respectively. *Each sex* should be able to represent both possibilities" (117).

3. My discussion of Irigaray here is based largely on "Sexual Difference," the introductory essay in *An Ethics of Sexual Difference* (5–19). The key terms I have used from Irigaray—angel, mucus, lips—all emerge from this essay and are key components of Irigaray's vision of sexual difference. The mucous membranes are the site of a "communion" between lovers (19); angels are "messengers of ethics" that represent "a sexuality that has never been incarnated" (16); the paired lips of the woman's body provide a model of the ethical relationship, for they "do not assimilate, reduce, or swallow up" (18). See chapter 1, note 21, for further references to these figures.

4. Irigaray's ethics of sexual difference is in many ways a response to the philosophical tradition, particularly Emmanuel Levinas's work on ethics. She writes that Levinas's view of love fails to reach "the transcendence of the other which becomes im-mediate ecstasy in me and with him—or her. For Levinas, the distance is always maintained with the other in the experience of love . . . This autistic, egological, solitary love does not correspond to the shared outpouring, to the loss of boundaries which takes place for both lovers when they cross the boundary of the skin into the mucous membranes of the body, leaving the circle which encloses my solitude" ("Questions to Emmanuel Levinas" 180). Her description of the crossing of the boundary between lovers in this passage could be a description of the genuine encounter between the narrator and Louise at the end of the novel.

5. Although these numerous affairs are presented comically, there is a kind of urgency about some of them that indicates the narrator's greater investment. The narrator seems crushed when one lover, Bathsheba, returns to her husband. With Jacqueline, she consciously seeks out a long-term, committed relationship, and when she leaves Jacqueline for Louise (with guilty doubts about her choice), Jacqueline's revenge is brutal and devastating.

6. See 89, 106, 118, 124–25 for other passages on writing on the body.

7. In "The Fecundity of the Caress," Irigaray writes, "The other cannot be transformed into discourse, fantasies, or dreams. It is impossible for me to substitute any other, thing or god, for the other—because of this touching of and by him, which my body remembers" (*An Ethics* 216). This cautionary remark certainly bears on the narrator's deep involvement in finding a stand-in for Louise in the form of a scientific knowledge of the body.

8. The body of the anatomy textbook is more likely to be a "universal" male body than a female body, except in the chapter on reproduction.

9. Several critics and commentators on the novel see this section in a very different light. Christy L. Burns sees the narrator's writing in this section as "playful and erotic" (11). She also claims that the narrator counteracts the clinical textbook language though her own rewriting of it (Burns refers to "the narrator's own resistance to the callousness of that language and her/his attempt to fantasize Louise's presence into being" [11]). Laura Reed-Morrison reads the section in a similar way, writing that "the narrator . . . rewrites sterile medical language as something transcendently personal" (1). See Carolyn Allen, *Following Djuna* 76 and Daphne M. Kutzer 143 for similar comments on this section. Taking a different approach, I argue that a strong undercurrent of violence marks this section, because the model of the anatomy textbook is not just "clinical" but dehumanizing on several levels, and the narrator's language is taken over by it.

10. While working in the British Museum, the narrator reflects on a visual image of a pilgrim and a maze in an illuminated manuscript in which these figures illustrate the letter "L." The narrator asks herself, "How would the pilgrim try through the maze, the maze so simple to angels and birds. I tried to fathom the path for a long time but I was caught at dead ends . . . I gave up and shut the book, forgetting that the first word had been Love" (88). Again, at this stage, the narrator is simply not up to the task of finding her way through the maze of love, either literally or, as here, figuratively.

11. Louise's angelic status makes her a figure of the fluid boundary as much as the narrator is through her undeclared gender. In chapter 4, I discussed Irigaray's figure of the angel, which stands for the merging of opposed terms and the crossing of boundaries on many levels. See *Written on the Body* 54, 131, 160 for references to Louise as an angel.

12. For readings of the ending as fantastic, see Burns 14–15 and Allen, *Following Djuna* 71–72.

13. This passage alludes to John Donne's "The Good Morrow" and "The Sun Rising."

14. This could also imply that the narrator's penis is too small to be caught in the trap. There are other suggestions that the narrator could be male, such as his/her boyfriend "Crazy Frank," who wears nipple rings in an attempt to be "deeply butch" (92). Crazy Frank seems like a gay man, thus leading the reader to consider whether the narrator might be a bisexual man. Most of the evidence, however, points to the narrator being female.

15. For one example of such an interview, see Winterson, "I fear insincerity," where she says that *Written on the Body* is based on her affair with her former agent, Pat Kavanagh. Allen cites similar reasons for read-

ing the narrator as a woman (*Following Djuna* 48–49). She also situates the narrator's unspecified sex in the context of fear of loss, which is the key to her argument about women's fiction in the Barnes tradition. The unspecified sex works to undercut the similarity of the lovers' bodies, which threatens "loss of boundaries" in the psychological sense (49).

16. These passages may be read in another sense as well, however. Although I maintain that the narrator is a woman, it is possible to imagine such passages being written about a certain kind of relationship between a man and a woman. This would be the sort of true union between the sexes that Irigaray describes in the context of wonder.

17. Winterson reserves the genderless status for her narrator: all the other characters are decidedly male or female.

18. Indeed, the position of the universal is not just available to men but is by its very definition a male position, as the use of "he" in English as the "universal" pronoun attests.

19. Burns notes the similarities between *Written on the Body* and Wittig's *The Lesbian Body*. I will be exploring the connections between the novel and Wittig's critical writing in *The Straight Mind*. All further references are to this text. Kutzer mentions in passing that *Written on the Body* "comes quite close" to Wittig's call for a "minority point-of-view that becomes truly universal," but she discusses neither the means of achieving this nor the ramifications of it in the novel (140).

20. Wittig writes that "straight society is based on the necessity of the different/other at every level . . . what is the different/other if not the dominated?" (29).

21. This statement should be qualified. The narrator makes several references to past boyfriends, but far more to girlfriends. Like Robin Vote in *Nightwood* and J in *The Talking Room*, her sexuality is not easily contained. All three women are bisexual in terms of their sexual practice but seem to be lesbian in terms of identity and desire.

22. We learn more about Elgin than we do about Louise or the narrator (of whom we learn nothing at all). We learn of his family and childhood, his career path, his sexual interests (masochism), and the history of his relationship with Louise.

23. My experience of teaching the novel to undergraduates is telling. Many of my students were preoccupied with "finding out" the narrator's "real gender," to the point of asking me if Winterson revealed what it "really was" in interviews.

24. In her essay on the convergence of feminism and postmodernism in three of Winterson's novels (see 143, 149), Laura Doan addresses the issue of Winterson's female characters usurping masculine power in *Oranges Are Not the Only Fruit* and *The Passion*. In my reading, the universal voice of

the narrator in *Written on the Body* has a similar function. Doan's readings of Winterson's various strategies for challenging the gender binary and the institution of heterosexuality (including parody, cross-dressing, and grafting) are similar to my readings of Barnes and Hauser in particular. I see my reading of the narrative voice in *Written on the Body* as a further stage in what Doan calls Winterson's creation of "a sexual politics of heterogeneity and a vision of hybridized gender constructions outside an either/or proposition" (154).

Afterword

1. For Judith Butler's commentary on Irigaray's and Wittig's respective positions, see *Gender Trouble* 18.

2. As Wittig writes, "[I]t is oppression that creates sex and not the contrary. The contrary would be to say that sex creates oppression or to say that the cause (origin) of oppression is to be found in sex itself, in a natural division of the sexes preexisting (or outside of) society" (2).

3. Wittig claims that "lesbian is the only category I know of which is beyond the categories of sex (woman and man), because the designated subject (lesbian) is *not* a woman, either economically, or politically, or ideologically. For what makes a woman is a specific social relation to a man" (20).

WORKS CITED

Allen, Carolyn. "'Dressing the Unknowable in the Garments of the Known': The Style of Djuna Barnes's *Nightwood*." *Women's Language and Style*. Ed. Douglas Butturf and Edmund L. Epstein. Akron, OH: U of Akron P, 1978. 106–18.

———. *Following Djuna: Women Lovers and the Erotics of Loss*. Bloomington: Indiana UP, 1996.

———. "Writing toward *Nightwood*: Djuna Barnes' Seduction Stories." Broe 54–65.

Barnes, Djuna. *Djuna Barnes's Nightwood: The Original Version and Related Drafts*. Ed. Cheryl J. Plumb. Normal, IL: Dalkey Archive Press, 1995.

———. *Nightwood*. 1937. New York: New Directions, 1961.

Baxter, Charles. "A Self-Consuming Light: *Nightwood* and the Crisis of Modernism." *Journal of Modern Literature* 3 (1974): 1175–87.

Bennett, Paula. "Critical Clitoridectomy: Female Sexual Imagery and Feminist Psychoanalytic Theory." *Signs* 18 (1993): 235–59.

Benstock, Shari. *Women of the Left Bank: Paris, 1900–1940*. Austin: U of Texas P, 1986.

Bowlby, Rachel. *Virginia Woolf*. Oxford: Basil Blackwell, 1988.

Broe, Mary Lynn, ed. *Silence and Power: A Reevaluation of Djuna Barnes*. Carbondale: Southern Illinois UP, 1991.

Burns, Christy L. "Fantastic Language: Jeanette Winterson's Recovery of the Postmodern World." *Contemporary Literature*. 37. 2 (1996): 20 pp. 7 Sept. 1998. *Searchbank* <http://web7.searchbank.com/infotrac/session/844/241/111859w7/31xrn_3>

Butler, Judith. "Against Proper Objects." *differences* 6. 2–3 (1994): 1–26.

———. *Bodies That Matter: On the Discursive Limits of Sex*. New York: Routledge, 1993.

———. *Gender Trouble: Feminism and the Subversion of Identity*. New York: Routledge, 1990.

177

Caserio, Robert L. "Supreme Court Discourse vs. Homosexual Fiction." *South Atlantic Quarterly* 88.1 (1989): 267–99.

Caughie, Pamela L. *Virginia Woolf and Postmodernism: Literature in Quest and Question of Itself.* Urbana: U of Illinois P, 1991.

——. "Virginia Woolf's Double Discourse." *Discontented Discourses: Feminism/Textual Intervention/Psychoanalysis.* Ed. Marleen S. Barr and Richard Feldstein. Urbana: U of Illinois P, 1989.

Chauncey, George. "From Sexual Inversion to Homosexuality: Medicine and the Changing Conception of Female Deviance." *Salmagundi* 58–59 (1982–83): 114–46.

Derrida, Jacques. *Dissemination.* Trans. Barbara Johnson. Chicago: U of Chicago P, 1981.

——. *Margins of Philosophy.* Trans. Alan Bass. Chicago: U of Chicago P, 1982.

——. *Of Grammatology.* Trans. Gayatri Chakravorty Spivak. Baltimore: Johns Hopkins UP, 1976.

——. *Spurs/Eperons.* Trans. Barbara Harlow. Chicago: U of Chicago P, 1979.

——. "Women in the Beehive: A Seminar with Jacques Derrida." *Men in Feminism.* Ed. Alice Jardine and Paul Smith. New York: Methuen, 1987. 189–203.

Derrida, Jacques, and Christie V. McDonald. "Choreographies." *diacritics* 12 (1982): 66–76.

Di Battista, Maria. *Virginia Woolf's Major Novels: The Fables of Anon.* New Haven: Yale UP, 1980.

Dick, Susan. "I Remembered, I Forgotten: Bernard's Final Soliloquy in *The Waves.*" *Modern Language Studies* 13.3 (1983): 38–52.

Doan, Laura. "Jeanette Winterson's Sexing the Postmodern." *The Lesbian Postmodern.* Ed. Laura Doan. New York: Columbia UP, 1994. 137–55.

Doane, Mary Ann. "Film and the Masquerade: Theorising the Female Spectator." *Screen* 23.3–4 (1982): 74–87.

Fleishman, Avrom. *Virginia Woolf: A Critical Reading.* Baltimore: Johns Hopkins UP, 1975.

Freud, Sigmund. "Femininity." *The Standard Edition of the Complete Psychological Works.* Trans. James Strachey. 24 vols. London: Hogarth, 1953. 22: 112–35.

——. "Mourning and Melancholia." *General Psychological Theory.* Ed. Philip Rieff. New York: Collier, 1963. 164–79.

——. "Three Essays on the Theory of Sexuality." *The Standard Edition.* 1953. 7: 125–245.

Friedman, Ellen G., and Miriam Fuchs, eds. *Breaking the Sequence: Women's Experimental Fiction*. Princeton: Princeton UP, 1989.

Friedman, Susan Stanford. "Lyric Subversion of Narrative in Women's Writing: Virginia Woolf and the Tyranny of Plot." *Reading Narrative: Form, Ethics, Ideology*. Ed. James Phelan. Columbus: Ohio State UP, 1989. 162–85.

Gerstenberger, Donna. "The Radical Narrative of Djuna Barnes's *Nightwood*." Friedman and Fuchs 129–39.

Gilbert, Sandra M., and Susan Gubar. *Sexchanges*. Vol. 2 of *No Man's Land: The Place of the Woman Writer in the Twentieth Century*. New Haven: Yale UP, 1989.

Graham, J. W. "Point of View in *The Waves*: Some Services of the Style." *Virginia Woolf: A Collection of Criticism*. Ed. Thomas S. W. Lewis. New York: McGraw-Hill, 1975. 94–112.

Grosz, Elizabeth A. *Sexual Subversions: Three French Feminists*. Sydney: Allen, 1989.

Guiguet, Jean. *Virginia Woolf and Her Works*. Trans. Jean Stewart. New York: Harcourt Brace Jovanovich, 1965.

Harris, Andrea "'Bare Things': Returning to the Senses in Virginia Woolf's *The Waves*." *LIT: Literature, Interpretation, Theory* 7.4 (1997): 339–50.

Hauser, Marianne. *Dark Dominion*. New York: Random House, 1947.

———. *A Lesson in Music*. Austin: U of Texas P, 1964.

———. *The Memoirs of the Late Mr. Ashley: An American Comedy*. Los Angeles: Sun and Moon, 1986.

———. *Prince Ishmael*. New York: Stein and Day, 1963.

———. *The Talking Room*. New York: Fiction Collective, 1976.

Henke, Suzette A. "Virginia Woolf's *The Waves*: A Phenomenological Reading." *Neophilologus* 73 (1989): 461–72.

Hussey, Mark. *The Singing of the Real World: The Philosophy of Virginia Woolf's Fiction*. Columbus: Ohio State UP, 1986.

———. *Virginia Woolf A to Z*. New York: Oxford UP, 1995.

Irigaray, Luce. *An Ethics of Sexual Difference*. Trans. Carolyn Burke and Gillian C. Gill. Ithaca: Cornell UP, 1993.

———. "Questions to Emmanuel Levinas." *The Irigaray Reader*. Ed. Margaret Whitford. Oxford: Blackwell, 1991. 178–89.

———. *Sexes and Genealogies*. Trans. Gillian C. Gill. New York: Columbia UP, 1993.

———. *Speculum of the Other Woman*. Trans. Gillian C. Gill. Ithaca: Cornell UP, 1985.

————. *This Sex Which Is Not One*. Trans. Catherine Porter. Ithaca: Cornell UP, 1985.

Jardine, Alice A. *Gynesis: Configurations of Woman and Modernity*. Ithaca: Cornell UP, 1985.

Jardine, Alice, and Paul Smith, eds. *Men in Feminism*. New York: Methuen, 1987.

Kelley, Alice Van Buren. *The Novels of Virginia Woolf: Fact and Vision*. Chicago: U of Chicago P, 1973.

Kessler, Suzanne J., and Wendy McKenna. *Gender: An Ethnomethodological Approach*. New York: Wiley, 1978.

Kutzer, M. Daphne. "The Cartography of Passion: Cixous, Wittig, and Winterson. *Re-Naming the Landscape*." Ed. Jurgen Kleist and Bruce A. Butterfield. New York: Lang, 1994. 133–45.

Lee, Judith. "*Nightwood*: 'The Sweetest Lie'." Broe 207–18.

Marcus, Jane. "Laughing at Leviticus: *Nightwood* as Woman's Circus Epic." Broe 221–50.

Martin, Biddy. "Sexualities Without Genders and Other Queer Utopias." *diacritics* 24. 2–3 (1994): 104–21.

McCaffery, Larry. *Some Other Frequency: Interviews with American Authors*. Philadelphia: U of Pennsylvania P, 1996.

McCaffery, Larry, and Sinda Gregory. "An Interview with Marianne Hauser." *Mississippi Review* 20.1–2 (1991): 120–30.

McConnell, Frank D. "'Death Among the Apple Trees': *The Waves* and the World of Things." *Virginia Woolf: A Collection of Critical Essays*. Ed. Claire Sprague. Englewood Cliffs, NJ: Prentice-Hall, 1971. 117–29.

Michel, Frann. "Displacing Castration: *Nightwood*, *Ladies Almanack*, and Feminine Writing." *Contemporary Literature* 30 (1989): 33–58.

Miko, Stephen J. "Reflections on *The Waves*: Virginia Woolf at the Limits of Her Art." *Criticism* 30.1 (1988): 63–90.

Minow-Pinkney, Makiko. *Virginia Woolf and the Problem of the Subject*. Brighton, England: Harvester, 1987.

Modleski, Tania. *Feminism Without Women: Culture and Criticism in a "Postfeminist" Age*. New York: Routledge, 1991.

Naremore, James. *The World Without a Self: Virginia Woolf and the Novel*. New Haven: Yale UP, 1973.

Newton, Esther. *Mother Camp: Female Impersonators in America*. 1972. Chicago: U of Chicago P, 1979.

Parker, Patricia. *Literary Fat Ladies: Rhetoric, Gender, Property*. New York: Methuen, 1987.

Pochoda, Elizabeth. "Style's Hoax: A Reading of Djuna Barnes's *Nightwood*." *Twentieth Century Literature* 22 (1976): 179–91.

Porritt, Ruth. "Surpassing Derrida's Deconstructed Self: Virginia Woolf's Poetic Disarticulation of the Self." *Women's Studies* 21 (1992): 323–38.

Reed-Morrison, Laura. Rev. of *Written on the Body*, by Jeanette Winterson. *Chicago Review* 40.4 (1994): 4 pp. *Searchbank*. 21 Aug. 1998 <http://sbweb3.med.iacnet.com/infotrac/session/467/848/4040880/18?xrn_19

Rilke, Rainer Maria. *Duino Elegies and the Sonnets to Orpheus*. Trans. A. Poulin, Jr. Boston: Houghton Mifflin, 1977.

Rivers, J. E. "The Myth and Science of Homosexuality in *A la recherche du temps perdu*." *Homosexualities and French Literature*. Ed. George Stambolian and Elaine Marks. Ithaca: Cornell UP, 1979. 262–78.

Riviere, Joan. "Womanliness as a Masquerade." *Psychoanalysis and Female Sexuality*. Ed. Hendrik M. Ruitenbeek. New Haven: College and University, 1966. 209–20.

Roof, Judith. "The Match in the Crocus: Representations of Lesbian Sexuality." *Discontented Discourses: Feminism/Textual Intervention/Psychoanalysis*. Ed. Marleen S. Barr and Richard Feldstein. Urbana: U of Illinois P, 1989. 100–116.

Rosenman, Ellen Bayuk. "Sexual Identity and *A Room of One's Own*: Secret Economies in Virginia Woolf's Feminist Discourse." *Signs* 14 (1989): 634–50.

Rubin, Gayle. "Thinking Sex: Notes for a Radical Theory of the Politics of Sexuality." *Pleasure and Danger: Exploring Female Sexuality*. Ed. Carole S. Vance. Boston: Routledge and Kegan Paul, 1984. 267–319.

———. "The Traffic in Women: Notes on the 'Political Economy' of Sex." *Toward an Anthropology of Women*. Ed. Rayna R. Reiter. New York: Monthly Review Press, 1975. 157–210.

Russo, Mary. "Female Grotesques: Carnival and Theory." *Feminist Studies/Critical Studies*. Ed. Teresa de Lauretis. Bloomington: Indiana UP, 1986. 213–29.

Schor, Naomi. "This Essentialism Which Is Not One: Coming to Grips with Irigaray." *differences* 1.2 (1989): 38–58.

Sedgwick, Eve Kosofsky. *Epistemology of the Closet*. Berkeley: U of California P, 1990.

Singer, Alan. "The Horse Who Knew Too Much: Metaphor and the Narrative of Discontinuity in *Nightwood*." *Contemporary Literature* 25.1 (1984): 66–87.

Spivak, Gayatri Chakravorty. "Displacement and the Discourse of Woman." *Displacement: Derrida and After.* Ed. Mark Krupnick. Bloomington: Indiana UP, 1983. 169–95.

Stewart, Garrett. "Catching the Stylistic D/rift: Sound Defects in Woolf's *The Waves.*" *ELH* 54.2 (1987): 421–61.

Tyler, Carol-Anne. "Playing with(out) the Signifier." Rev. of *Gynesis*, by Alice Jardine. *Novel* 21 (1987): 103–6.

Warminski, Andrzej. *Readings in Interpretation: Hölderlin, Hegel, Heidegger.* Minneapolis: U of Minnesota P, 1986.

Warner, Eric. *The Waves.* Cambridge: Cambridge UP, 1987.

Whitford, Margaret. *The Irigaray Reader.* Oxford: Blackwell, 1991.

———. *Luce Irigaray: Philosophy in the Feminine.* New York: Routledge, 1991.

Willis, Sharon. Rev. of *Gynesis: Configurations of Woman and Modernity,* by Alice A. Jardine. *diacritics* 18.1 (1988): 29–41.

Winterson, Jeanette. "I fear insincerity." With Michelle Field. *Publishers Weekly* Mar. 20, 1995: 1 p. *Searchbank.* CD-ROM. Aug. 1997.

———. *Written On the Body.* Toronto: Vintage, 1992.

Wittig, Monique. *The Straight Mind and Other Essays.* Boston: Beacon, 1992.

Woolf, Virginia. *A Room of One's Own.* 1929. New York: Harcourt Brace, 1957.

———. "Craftsmanship." *Collected Essays.* 4 vols. New York: Harcourt, Brace and World, 1967. 2: 248–51.

———. *The Diary of Virginia Woolf.* Ed. Anne Olivier Bell. 5 vols. New York: Harcourt Brace Jovanovich, 1979–85.

———. "Mr. Bennett and Mrs. Brown." *Collected Essays.* 4 vols. New York: Harcourt, Brace and World, 1967. 1: 319–37.

———. "Modern Fiction." *Collected Essays.* 4 vols. New York: Harcourt, Brace and World, 1967. 2: 103–10.

———. *The Waves.* 1931. New York: Harcourt Brace Jovanovich, 1959.

Ziarek, Ewa. "'Taking Chances': The Feminine Genealogy of Style in Marianne Hauser's *The Talking Room.*" *Contemporary Literature* 33 (1992): 480–501.

INDEX

Allen, Carolyn, 163n. 5, 164n. 9, 174n. 9, 174–75n. 15
androgyny, 86, 157n. 2, 162n. 36, 166n. 26, 168n. 7; and anonymity, 32
angel, 22, 98, 142, 151, 157n. 21; and boundary crossing, 174n. 11; in Irigaray, 126–27, 172n. 36, 173n. 3; and other sexes, 125–28; in Rilke, 172n. 34; as terrifying, 171–72n. 33; and writing, 172n. 37
anonymity, 31–32; and dreams, 73; and identity, xiv; and language, 42; and love, 67; privileging of, 33

Barnes, Djuna, 22–23, 126; on gender, 166n. 24, 176n. 24; *Nightwood*, xii–xiii, 63–95, 114, 124, 128, 129–30, 151, 156n. 16, 157n. 21, 159n. 11, 168n. 6, 170n. 20, 171n. 24; on sex, 164n. 10
Baxter, Charles, 80, 163n. 3, 165n. 19
Bennett, Paula, 169n. 15
Benstock, Shari, 153n. 3, 163n. 3
body, 21, 173n. 8; alienation from, 31; female, 11; and language, 36; and sex/gender, 74; violation of, 136, 138–40
border, xiv
boundary: crossing of, 143, 144; fluid, 137
Bowlby, Rachel, 158–59n. 8
Broe, Mary Lynn, 163n. 3
Burne-Jones, Edward, 141
Burns, Christy L., 174n. 9, 175n. 19
Butler, Judith, 1, 76, 165n. 21; *Bodies That Matter*, 155n. 9, 171n. 27; on drag, 18, 156n. 17, 165n. 23; on gay/lesbian identity, 171n. 23; on gay/lesbian studies, 154n. 2; on gender identity, 167n. 32, 170n. 21, 170n. 22, 171n. 28; on Kristeva, 159n. 10; on melancholy, 166n. 29; on mimesis, 156n. 14; performative gender, xiii, 2, 3, 13, 18–21; on sex 164n. 10; on subject, 25, 43; on third gender, 88; on Wittig, 156n. 18

Caserio, Robert L., 167n. 1
Caughie, Pamela L., 153n. 4, 168n. 7
character, 27, 28
Chauncey, George, 162n. 2, 165n. 22
chiasmus, 64, 85–87, 89–90, 166n. 24
Cixous, Hélène, 36, 165n. 20
clitoris, 110–11

deconstruction, 9, 17
Derrida, Jacques, 2, 10–11, 160n. 13; on the female body, 6, 8; and the feminine, 155n. 9; hymen, 5–9, 13, 155n. 9; on woman, 6, 8–10, 15–16
Di Battista, Maria, 158n. 5
Dick, Susan, 158n. 6
difference, 62, 128, 151; and oppression, 150; in Woolf, xi
dilatio, 107, 169n. 11
displacement, 6–10, 27, 60–62, 162n. 1; and male theorist, 2; and masculine subject, 162n. 37; and woman, 16
Doan, Laura, 175–76n. 24
Doane, Mary Ann, 156n. 14
Donne, John, 174n. 13

183